The
'Her'story
of
Davidisms

The 'Her'story of Davidisms

My Straight-Shooting Answers to 30 Years of Career Questions People Have Asked Me

PATRICIA DAVID

PICARD
PRESS

Published 2021
Printed in the United States of America
Paperback ISBN: 978-1-7376126-0-5
E-ISBN: 978-1-7376126-1-2
Library of Congress Control Number: 2021919359

Picard Press
New Jersey
picardpressinfo@gmail.com

Book design by Stacey Aaronson
Printed in the USA

In memory of my parents, Thomas and Jeanette LeBlanc.
Your sacrifice was duly paid.

For my husband, Curt, who put up with me while
I was advising others.

And for my children, Sammy and BK,
for being easy to raise.

"Did you eat?"
—Jeanette LeBlanc

Contents

Introduction

For as long as I can remember—usually shortly after I have given a speech, moderated a panel, or given people advice on what they should do with their career or life in general—someone has said to me, "You should write a book." Well, folks, I'm now retired. And after thirty-plus years of hearing this request, and since I've had more time of late, I have finally done it!

So, here it is—a (hopefully) approachable, fun, and easy-to-digest series of thoughts, sayings, and advice I have given to a slew of people (some repeatedly) over the years that have come to be known as "Davidisms."

I had a lot of title choices for this book, but I landed on *The 'Her'story of Davidisms* for two reasons. 1) The diversity play on the word 'her'story versus *his*tory. Get it? *Her* versus *his*. And 2) *The Book of David*, which my cousin Perry thought would be a good title (and I do love Denzel Washington and his acting in *The Book of Eli*), sounded a bit religious and would probably not be the first book someone picked up looking for career or life advice. I figured if they had to choose between my *Book of David* and the Bible, I doubted mine would end up in the cart! So there you have it: *The 'Her'story of Davidisms* was born and bound.

Here's the thing: the words you are about to read are my thoughts and personal views on managing one's career based upon what I have learned, what I have observed, what I have heard others say, or things I have experienced in my professional career and life in general. I have tried my best to recall the numerous scenarios under which I gave advice and blurted out other Davidisms that have stood the test of time in the hope that this collection of ideas, thoughts, and actions will bolster you when faced with questions such as:

"How do I keep my career moving?"

"How do I keep myself motivated?"

"How do I find a mentor?"

"Do I need to quit to get a raise?"

"How do I get to the next level?"

(By the way, this question is really code for "How do I get promoted?" And if this is what you want to know, then I want you to think about why you aren't clearer about asking the question. Yes, it drives me nuts when people beat around the bush!)

With this in mind, remember that clarity is king (or should I say *queen*)!

I'll be honest: I have found it weird to have all kinds of people ask for my opinion or advice, because I am not an expert in career management, nor am I a professional motivational speaker (even though I do motivate people when I speak!). When I ask people why they are asking *me* of all the people they could ask for guidance, I repeatedly receive the following answers: "You don't sugar coat." "You are very direct and honest." "You are empathetic but unapologetic." "Your advice is candid and easy to follow." I tell you this to make sure you know this book is not founded on any fancy research, or expert analysis, or anything that would stand up to scrutiny. It is purely grounded in my views and values based on my experience, so please, take it for what it's worth—and know I'm imparting my advice to you because in many cases, it has worked. (Too bad I wasn't charging for it at the time!)

I hope the points I share resonate with you and give you guidance and clarity for what ails you. Since people have told me that the way I verbalize these tidbits is what makes them memorable, I hope you'll appreciate my style—I tell the truth, raw and honest, direct and straight, without any apology, even if it hurts or stings. In fact, I always say, "I'll tell you the truth, but don't get upset with me if you don't like it." Yes, some of my thoughts might seem unconventional and hard core, but they're also practical and have proven to set people on the track they desire.

Who Is This Book For?

I like to think this book is for anyone, but I know that's probably wishful thinking, so let me be more specific. Yes, this book can apply to anyone in business, but I have included a section for ladies only, one for leaders, and even a few pointers for summer interns with their brand-new suits. (If this is you, may I just tell you here and now to make sure you take the tag off the sleeve, as well as snip off the little X string on the back of the skirt or jacket.) I also included some one-liners and a few real-life conversations I have had with people. (Don't worry if you are reading these and realize this is you and I talking—trust me, _____ , I did not put your name in this book.)

So, if you are curious how to get ahead in your career, if you are working hard but not moving, if you are able to do your job but don't feel satisfied or fulfilled after you do it, if you are curious how to find a mentor, or if you simply have questions you hope I have the answers to, this book might be just what you've been looking for. If not, feel free to regift it.

Breakfast of Champions: Davidisms Warmup

Knowing I'm not a gal who beats around the bush, you won't be surprised that we're going to jump right in with some of my most notable snippets of advice. Think of this as the appetizer before the big meal. I hope you are hungry!

*Attitude: We should all have one.
Just make sure it's a positive one.*

Most of the time, when people say he/she has an attitude, it's taken negatively, right? But for me, I see it as a positive. Sure, have an attitude—but make sure it's one of happiness, joy, positivity, and confidence. If you're going to have a disposition about life, these are excellent choices. The power of positive thinking is real and I believe in it. I know without a doubt that having an enthusiastic attitude makes me feel good inside. So if *you* want to feel good inside, have an attitude that follows you everywhere. When people say "Pat has an attitude," it makes me smile. That means the happy, joyful, positive, confident me showed up.

☀

Smile. It increases your face value.

I don't know about you, but it sure feels a lot better to smile than to frown, and your face looks a lot better too.

☀

Don't overstay your welcome, or you won't be welcome to overstay again.

As a kid growing up in the Bronx, our house was known as Grand Central Station. This was because many relatives coming to America from the Commonwealth of Dominica were welcome to stay at our house while they got themselves settled ("settled" being code for getting their green card). But my dad would always remind them: "Don't overstay your welcome, or you won't be welcome to overstay again." Wise words if you ask me. This is especially applicable when it comes to a job or a position. Know when to leave. (In corporate America, it's known as a "blocker." More about this later.)

☀

Be careful of the company who keeps you.

You have heard the saying, "Be careful of the company you keep." But as I get wiser, I think it should be reworded to say, "Be careful of the company **who keeps you**.

Let me paint you an example.

A person you just met says they heard about you from someone they know, someone who is good friends with you and knows you well. Upon hearing the name, you think: *This person has attended a few of my events and heard me speak, we have had pleasant hallway conversations, and they know my name because it's on the headline of the events, but I honestly couldn't pick them out in a crowd.*

Do you see where this is going? Just by this person implying they know me or is friends with me raises their brand, which might be good for them but not so good for me. Since I don't know them well enough to gauge that meter, I take responsibility right away and tell the person I'm meeting with something like this: "Is that so? I only met so and so once and haven't really interacted with them. So although we may have met a few times and exchanged pleasantries, they're probably stretching the truth about our relationship by saying they're my friend."

Like I said, I am very careful about the company that keeps me. I don't want people to be hanging off me like a barnacle on a whale, and I doubt you do either! So if this happens to you, grab my response above and manage your brand—*you*. This tactic accomplishes two things. 1) It clarifies the relationship; and 2) It makes the person you are speaking to aware you won't put up with having them try to pull a fast one on you.

☀

Don't chase your dream – catch it already!

Why do people say to "chase your dreams"? Wouldn't it be more worthwhile if you caught and realized them instead? So let's stop saying "chase your dream" and catch it already. Deal?

☀

Make a difference every day.

I'd love to make this into a snappy acronym, but Make a Difference becomes MAD, and I don't like telling anyone to get mad every day. So for this one, I'm confident you can remember this short phrase and apply it to your daily life. All you have to do is this: From the time you wake up in the morning, try to make a difference with every being and item you encounter. It doesn't have to be something magnificent; it can be something small, like a smile to a stranger, or tenderness toward a child or pet, or putting something back where you found it. But wake up with the mindset of making a difference every single day, knowing you create a ripple effect of kindness, respect, and goodness that others will appreciate.

Don't come to work to make friends or enemies.

This is an important Davidism, especially for women in business. Why? Because women are naturally maternal and want to be liked. So when we are working on a team, solving a problem, or simply interacting with people day to day, we are careful how we speak or what we say because we don't want someone to not like us. As a result, we hesitate to speak our mind. Instead, we tend to pause and question, *If I say this or do that, will people like me? Or will people be my friend or foe?* When this happens, we get off our game and lose focus, which takes away from our ability to think clearly, to deliver, and to execute.

My advice is, as best as you can, always focus on the problem you are working on as the centerpiece when making *all* of your decisions. If your actions are in line with the temperament you need to solve the problem, trust me: real business people know this. They don't want to be your friend and see smiles; what they want is comfort that you can solve the problem, handle issues and crises, and move forward. In short, it's *not* about making friends or enemies. It never is, was, or will be. It is about cultivating relationships, getting things done, and executing while not getting executed in the process!

I'll be honest, it took me a while to realize this because I grew up wanting to be liked. We all do. But having the mission of being liked in business does not get you anywhere—being respected does.

*Don't come to work to work –
come to work to network.*

Don't get me wrong: working is important, and you get paid to do it. But don't forget about the importance of *networking*—meeting people, developing relationships, and expanding your professional circle. To that end, take a percentage of your day, week, or month and make it a point to network with others. Expanding your network will have an impact on your net worth long term.

I remember when I got my first professional business job after college. When I received the offer in the mail, I was so excited. I shared it with my mom, and the advice she gave me was the best advice she had: "Get to work earlier than the boss, leave later than the boss, and don't get the boss mad." It sounded like pretty good advice at the time. So I did this for several years. I took on more than my fair share, was a pleasant teammate, and was happy to get my annual incremental increase. I always assumed the bosses knew how hard I worked and would in time determine when it would be my turn to get promoted.

At a certain point, I realized some of the people

who got hired when I did were getting promotions while I wasn't inching ahead at all. I thought to myself, *Hey, I work harder, I'm smarter, I don't make any noise, and I do great work. Why am I not moving up?* Well, when I picked my head up and observed what *they* were doing versus what *I* was doing, it was clear they were not only working, they were doing a whole lot of *networking.* I had spent years being enamored with watching people lean up against the wall in the hallway and talk to each other, or saunter over to someone's desk and chat, or attend various work events, or even —dare I say—go to lunch with each other even when they weren't hungry. But me? I was too busy working to do those things! Yet I began to see that these people were smart about getting others to know not just who they were, but what they were thinking, what they were capable of, and what potential they carried.

So, I continued to heed my mom's advice, but I used my time more wisely. I still got to the office early and left late, but I made sure it was more balanced between working and developing relationships, or working and attending company events, or working and getting involved in some extracurricular activities. The learning for me was to focus on all aspects of the job—which was not merely the *work*, but also the *network*. This one new habit helped me get my career to move at a faster pace. Although I think I would have eventually been successful in my career, this habit sped things up quite a bit.

:☼:

Your boss didn't give you a bad performance review – you earned it!

I hear this one a lot: "My boss gave me a bad review." Like it or not, you may have done a great job in your mind, but your boss had a different expectation, which perhaps didn't lead to the expected outcome. So if you want to get a better performance review from your boss, get specifics on their expectations long before that review ever happens.

:☼:

Don't worry about IF.

"If" is a silly little word that is very good at knocking you off your game. Here's why.

According to *Webster's Dictionary*, "if" is used to talk about the result or effect of something that *may* happen or be true. It's also used to discuss the imaginary result or effect of something that *did not* happen or that *is* or *was not* true.

Are you already sensing where we're going here? Why worry about something that may not happen or did not happen. What's the point of saying things like, "What if I get a new boss?" "What if I don't get promoted?" "What if the location of the job moves?" "What if I don't get the job offer?" The list goes on, right? If you can't help but ponder "ifs," then may I suggest rephrasing them as if they *are* actually going to happen:

What are my options when I get a new boss?

How will I pivot when I don't get the job offer?

What is my next move now that I'm not getting the promotion?

The point is that you don't want to lose yourself in all the endless possibilities, or worse, get roped into the hallway chatter of what others are saying, which can get into your head and nearly cripple your ability to function.

Don't get me wrong: it's a good idea to plan, but don't get caught up in all the combinations that *could* occur. Instead, focus on the reality or feasibility of your options and plan your strategy accordingly, basing your actions on facts, not emotions. It will save you a whole lot of time, trust me.

☀

Always eat from a fat cook.

Think about it: if you are asking someone for advice and that person is not a go-getter and is essentially stuck in the same job with a very limited network, and this person is advising you, get out of that kitchen. Always eat from a "fat" cook.

:ᐁ:

Don't treat people like YOU want to be treated.
Treat them like THEY want to be treated.

This one came to me after I read Stephen Covey's book *The 7 Habits of Highly Effective People*. All too often we hear "Treat people like you want to be treated," but in my view that's backwards. We should treat people like *they* want to be treated. How do we determine this? (drum roll) **Speak to people to find out how they want to be treated.** Yes, it requires a bit of work to find this out, which is why most of us take the short cut and treat people how *we* want to be treated. After all, it's easy to imagine, *If I want to be treated a certain way, it must be the right way because it's* my *way, so it stands to reason that I should treat others this way too, right?* Actually, no. If you think you can't go wrong with this angle, think again. You *can* go wrong.

Consider your beliefs, values, eating habits, etc. If you invited a friend over for dinner on Ramadan and they celebrate that holiday, you blew it. If you celebrate Christmas and your friends are Jewish, instead of wishing them Merry Christmas, you should wish them Happy Hanukkah. Or if a person is vegan or vegetarian, it would be nice to have something around your table your guests can eat. Cultural differences can, and also should, be considered, not just in terms of heritage months or religious holidays, but also when it comes to something as basic as offering a handshake or a hug. I think you get the picture. The learning here is to be knowledgable and respectful enough of others around you that you treat them the way *they* want to be treated. Bonus! It works both ways.

꿈

It's never the work, it's how you have to DO the work.

This Davidism can be applied in numerous ways, but the most relevant to me is when a person gets a job offer.

Let's say you receive an offer and it sounds perfect. The title is spot on, the pay is awesome; the location of the job and everything about it is a 10. You are on cloud nine because you found your perfect job. How lucky are you! And then it happens—you actually have to go to work and start that awesome-sounding, perfectly titled, salaried job with the flexibility you were hoping for.

The thing is, the perks that drew you to that position may wear off when you actually have to show up and *do* the work—under *their* conditions, in *their* environment, with *their* tools and processes, and so on. Now, not all wonderful-on-the-outside jobs turn into nightmares once you're on the inside. But what if you discover that the way things function don't suit you at all—because you forgot to ask this one question during the interview: HOW DOES THE WORK GET DONE? The bottom line: It may get done in the complete opposite work environment from what you excel in. I know about this all too well from my own experience. In fact, this Davidism was born from my experience working at Burger King when I was in college.

From my first day on the job, I found out that assembly-line and routine work does not bring out the best in me. I worked pretty fast, and I could make more burgers than anyone. But what I learned during my time there was that as much as I enjoy a good burger, I don't like repetition. At Burger King you have to make burgers over and over and over all day long with zero creativity. The burger goes between the bread, and the ketchup and pickle go on top of the burger. There is no strategic thinking or solving of complex problems (unless you think a complex problem is a customer who wants a burger without a bun!). Learning this about myself was truly an aha moment and a lesson I'm glad I grasped early in my career, because when I was offered a job after college, here's how I approached it.

The pay was nice, the title and salary were a good match for my experience and skills, and the job seemed perfect on paper. But during the interview, I asked the question mentioned above—along with two more very important ones:

"How does the work get done?"

"What is the routine of the department?"

"If I was on the team last month, what would I have been working on?"

I remember the hiring manager rattling off some specifics on how the team operates:

"All members must review new ideas with their peers before it is sent to management."

"All meetings have a pre-meeting."

"All emails we send need to have the manager cc'd."

"Every Monday the team meets to review in detail what is planned for the week."

"If you were on the team, you would have been helping prepare manuals for a board meeting, collating and packaging books to be sent out to senior management."

My face was nodding with a pleasant smile. My brain was thinking, *Oh, heck no. That is not the environment for me.*

Although the job and all of its attributes seemed perfect on paper, the reality was yes, I could have performed the tasks, but I would have been unhappy, and therefore not operating at my best. In short, that environment would have stifled me to death.

While some would find that job a perfect fit, I prefer a less structured environment. I actually thrive when there is chaos, confusion, and problem solving. Go figure!

So as you move into your profession, begin to understand what work environment brings out the best in you. Only you know the right answer. Then, seek out a job where this environment exists. The work will be challenging enough; if the environment is not a match, it will be twice as challenging for you to deliver.

So please, if you get an awesome job offer, ask the three questions on the prior page. The answers will help reinforce you are choosing an environment that brings out the best in you. I don't want you to have Burger King days—unless that's your thing, then have it your way. (wink)

:☼:

If I am carrying you, you better be carrying TWO.

This simply means that as a mentor, you always want to look behind you and help pull others up as you rise. In other words, as you get the opportunity to do great things, it's imperative that you take people with you and give them the opportunity you had—especially if you are a manager with the power and authority to move people up and give people exposure. It's called the "multiple effect" and the math is simple: If I'm carrying you, you better be carrying two.

☼

When in doubt, leave it out.
(courtesy of a mentor of mine named John)

"It" could be anything. If you have to ask if "it" belongs, or if you should include "it," or if "it" looks right, "it" probably does not belong. If "it" was a no-brainer, you would not torment and question "it." So whether "it" is a detail in a presentation or accessories for an outf "it," the Davidism is clear: When in doubt, leave "it" out. Most of the time, putting "it" in will not enhance wherever "it" was going anyhow.

☼

Not every question needs to be answered.

We as humans love to talk, and we love to ask questions—especially in a work setting (either because we want to appear smart or simply like to hear our own voices!). What we often don't like to do as much is answer questions—especially in a work setting.

Have you ever dreaded doing a presentation in front of a senior group of people? You knew your material and were confident in your data, but all you wanted was to get through it without being asked any questions?

I remember when I was a diversity officer heading into a board meeting for my annual update. I had spent a fair number of hours preparing, and even role-played questions that might come up. Just as I was cued to join the meeting, my boss looked at me and said, "Remember, not every question needs to be answered."

Wait—what?

I believed I always had to answer everyone's questions, that it was respectful and polite. Then he tossed these eight words out just as I was opening the door to the boardroom, with a room full of people staring at me.

I had only fifteen minutes to present the update, so I needed to stay focused and on point. And boom! A board member interrupts me and asks a question. Now, the "pre-eight-word-advice" Pat David would have taken the time to answer and subsequently been derailed and run out of time. But, remembering what my boss said, I instead replied, "That's a great question. I haven't thought of that and I'll consider it going forward." Boom, done! He was acknowledged, I responded in an appropriate way that was satisfactory, and I didn't lose any time answering him or get completely knocked off the topic of my presentation.

The point is, sometimes people like to fling questions out for any number of reasons: to hear themselves speak, to check the box that they participated, to get credit for saying something, to see how you handle a question. In this case, it was to throw out an idea.

So, the next time you are presenting or in a situation where someone asks a question, think fast and determine if it requires an answer or merely an acknowledgment. (This can apply to emails as well.)

As an aside, this Davidism does not, I repeat, does *not*, work at home. If you have a spouse or a partner, trust me—they expect every question they ask to be answered (sometimes repeatedly!).

☼

Play offense with your career, not defense.

This is one of my favorites because people are all too often in reaction mode when it comes to their careers. They are either reacting to a not-so-good performance review or the promotion that didn't come through, or beginning to worry about their job if the company has announced a merger, or reacting to relocation news, a reorganization, or whatever changes might occur in life.

When you think about it, most people spend a lot of time defending themselves against something that has already happened instead of preparing themselves while things are good in case something does happen.

Let's take a sports example (like baseball—Go, Yankees!). Usually, the winning team has a strong foundation comprised of pitchers, batters, fielders, coaches, managers, equipment, practice routines, etc. They go on the field with their plan to pitch, get strikeouts, hit the ball, and get on base. They don't just show up and wait to defend themselves on the field; they have their game plan and are operating from a position of strength.

In terms of managing your career and being on the offense, you also need a strong foundation in order to win, which I believe is composed of four things: financial stability, a strong professional network, exposure (making sure the right people know you and what your potential and capabilities are), and good health.

In short, offense is the best defense.

The question you should always be asking yourself is:

"Where would I go in good times, if everything was great and I wanted to move on?"

Then ask yourself:

"Do I have a relationship with someone who would hire me on the spot?"

"Do I have enough liquid cash for six months, or more?"

"Is my resume updated with my accomplishments?"

If you wake up every morning and feel good about the answers to these questions, you can feel assured you're on the offense—any news about change that came your way would be a lot easier to handle because you are operating with a strong foundation. I tell people to create a situation for themselves where they can go where they want when they want. It may take a lot of effort, but trust me, if you work toward this every day, you will be just like the Yankees—a winner! (Well, most of the time.)

Always BE ready so you don't have to GET ready.

This is similar to the previous Davidism but with a twist.

Imagine if you got a great opportunity to take on a new role, but your boss held you back longer than expected because you were the only person who knew how to perform a particular function. Or perhaps an overseas assignment came your way and you were unable to go because you didn't have a passport. Or maybe that outfit you wanted is on sale but you can't buy it because you didn't budget for it. For these and many other scenarios, "always be ready so you don't have to get ready" is applicable.

When it comes to your job or career, I want you to change how you think. That's right. I want you to go to work every day with the mindset of either leaving for a new position or retiring. I know you might love your job or be far from retiring, but stay with me. With this suggested mindset, would your affairs be in order? Are your processes documented? Are your teams trained to carry on your work without you? Is your successor ready and known by others? Does anyone in the department know what you know, or are you the only one?

For my lady readers, it's like having a go-bag when you're pregnant—you don't know when the baby is coming, but you know it *is* coming, so you are prepared to pick up and go without hesitation. In other words, you are ready so you don't have to get ready.

If you find yourself in a position of not being ready, you are boxing yourself in. When a new position or opportunity comes along, your manager will have the right to hold you back, say you can't transfer, or make the transfer timing months instead of weeks. I don't want that happening to you.

Here's another example.

As I moved up and was managing more people, I became really good at delegating and not doing any work that had to do with the operations of the department I was running. Don't get me wrong: I didn't just sit in the office and direct the work. But I always looked for opportunities to stay away from being the one critical cog in the wheel, or the only person who knew how to do something. This way, in case I needed to leave for whatever reason, I was not held back as the worker who needed to stay to ensure the job got done. This may not be so easy, depending on the position you have, but try as best you can to always have your processes documented, your files in order, and your contacts organized. Also, make sure someone else on your team knows how to perform a critical or frequent task, or generate a report you are responsible for. This not only gets *you* prepared, it can also be a great opportunity for someone on the team to expand their responsibilities.

So get yourself ready and put important things into place. And if you don't have a passport, get one—they last for ten years and are well worth the investment.

☀

Race against yourself, not anybody else.

As a teenager growing up in the Bronx, I remember envying what others had and found myself wishing and even praying I could have those same things: their car, clothes, money, popularity, hair, and even sometimes skin color. I spent far too much time trying to copy other people because I believed what I possessed was not as good, at least in my mind.

Luckily, when I started to work, I realized what a dumb cycle I'd gotten myself into (and my mom pounding into my head to never envy anyone also helped—ha!)—and so I began to race against *me*, not those around me. Changing my thinking and working on creating my own path eliminated a lot of wasted time and gave me clarity on not only being myself, but on being the best version of myself. This shift felt like I had taken a big, deep breath, and it felt good.

There are various ways I race against myself. I sometimes create silly tests, such as beating the repetitions from my exercise regimen from the day before, or exceeding my 10,000 steps one day, striving for 15,000 the next.

Ironically, if you race against others, you may be cutting yourself short because if you *can* do better than them, you will never know. Why? Because you have been following *their* path, which might be slower than your potential. How many times have you compared yourself to someone else, saying things like, "He was in my graduating class, and now he's a managing director making seven figures, and I'm just a vice president." He is not you and you are not him; the only thing in common is the day, place, and time you graduated. Do you actually think the entire class should all be at the same stage in their career? I bet not. So how is it you can pick one person who is ahead of you and think it's not fair in comparison to where you are? This is pure nonsense. And what about the people behind you? How do you think they feel?

That's what I believe my mom had in mind when she told me not to envy others—she knew in her heart I would hamper my potential if I did that. What a wise woman she was. (Thanks, Mom!)

The moral of the story? Too much time is spent

on keeping up with others, or following someone else's path. Don't waste time and energy following. Instead, strive to be the best version of *you*.

:☀:

Play checkers with your career by connecting with certain people and hopping over others.

You know how when you play checkers, you can hop over one disc to get to another, as long as it's in the line of the piece you want to get to? Well, you can apply this same strategy to your life as well. Who do you know who is connected to someone you want to know, and can that person introduce you? Once you have that person in your mind, go and make that connection!

:☀:

Don't just have a to-do list, also have a to-don't list.

I realize this may not be intuitive because the to-DO list is what most of us have used for decades to keep our lives organized. This is typically a great tool—I know that if I write something down or put it on my to-do list, it actually gets done. My to-do list not only keeps me on schedule, it's gratifying to look at the list after I check something off and feel a sense of accomplishment.

But even with the best-looking to-do list, during any normal workday there are things that can suck your time, create fatigue, lower your productivity, and result in long hours where your list looks the same from morning to evening. So how about putting together a list of things you *won't* do any more. Here are a few examples:

I will not let so and so come into my office and plop down in the chair and chat.

I will not turn on my computer for the first 15 minutes of work.

I will not go to lunch if I'm not hungry.

Are you getting the idea? If you did a time-elapsed study of where your time goes, you'd be able to craft your to-don't list, simply by seeing what activities and interruptions throw you off track.

When I did this several years ago for myself, I found out I was spending a lot of time catering to people who would saunter into my office and unload whatever was on their mind. Because they were in my office, I was a captive audience and could not escape (short of kicking them out or being a bad hostess, which was not in my nature because my momma raised me right!). After this realization, I added this to my to-don't list: *no more meetings in my office whenever possible.* I was fine with going to someone else's office for a meeting (so I could leave whenever I wanted to), but I no longer abided having impromptu meetings in mine. If you're wondering how I managed this, I told my administrative assistant that whenever possible, to hold all of my meetings in a conference room. I also removed the chairs from my office and used a stand-up desk so that if someone did saunter in, there was no place for them to sit, not to mention that standing gave the impression I was walking out when they were walking in.

So, spend some time thinking of the time wasters or low-productivity actions that occur during your day and create a to-don't list. Your time is precious. Manage it.

☀

If you are just wasting time and taking up space, stay home.

When you can predict your day and do your job without much thought, it's time to stay home. You are simply wasting time and taking up space. Let me explain.

When you reach the point where your job is "easy" by your standards, and you actually boast that you can do your job with your eyes closed, the best of you is not coming out. You are on auto-pilot, merely going through the motions. If you are serious about your career and want more challenges, this is not an "accomplishment" to celebrate. I consider this a self-inflicted wound—it's as close to career suicide as it gets. Sure, you can make noise and blame your boss for not giving you more challenging opportunities, which may be true, but there are a host of other things you can do to shake things up a bit.

The way I see it, you have two options:

1. Stay the course and wait to die, *or*
2. Choose to live.

If you choose to live, an easy tactic is to approach your job as if you were going to train your replacement. What would you tell them to do? Would you tell them to eliminate certain processes, or perhaps make sure they got onto a specific project?

I remember leaving a particular position and sitting down with the person replacing me. One of the first things I told them to do right away was to meet specific stakeholders and senior businesspeople who have respect in the organization, and to meet with them often to develop good relationships. I distinctly remember thinking as the words were coming out of my mouth, *I could have done my job ten times better if I took my own advice.*

I hope you don't make the same mistake.

So please don't boast about being able to do your job with your eyes closed. All that means is that you are not challenged and that your brain is not being used to its potential. To be blunt, you are essentially wasting time and taking up space.

The next time you get to this point—or better yet, *before* you get to this point—make it a habit to imagine you are training your replacement and think of what you would tell them, then start to do whatever that is.

What's on the menu gets eaten.

My friend, Robin, likes this one. What the saying conveys is that you want to make yourself known. When you attend a meeting, or even an informal gathering, say something, anything at all. For example, if you're at a town hall, you can raise your hand and say, "Hello, my name is _____ _____ , and I don't have a question but I wanted to echo what you said about such and such." This makes you visible and memorable, and people now attach your name with your face and your voice. It also shows that you're paying attention. Again, you don't always have to ask a question; you can simply reinforce a point.

When my daughter was in elementary school, I had a conference with her teacher. She said many nice things about my daughter—she wasn't cliquey, she interacted with all of the students, not just a few, and she achieved good grades. But there was one thing the teacher called her out on: participation—which she counted as 20 percent of the students' grade. In my daughter's case, she never raised her hand in class, and this was going to affect her final evaluation by the teacher.

That night when I got home, I told my daughter what the teacher said about her lack of participation.

"Ma," she said, "I don't raise my hand and ask any questions because I already know the answers."

I took that in, then said, "But your teacher doesn't know that!"

Even if it feels unnecessary, remember that speaking up makes you part of the session, instead of merely another person in the crowd. In the classroom, at a staff meeting, or even on a conference call, you can use the same tactic. Try it.

:☀:

It's better to give than to receive. (Courtesy of my mom, Jeanette LeBlanc)

This was a hard lesson when I was younger because my mom made sure we gave whenever we were able. For example, if I had one cookie, I had to give someone half. Her point was if you are blessed with talent, treasure, and time, you may have more than someone else and that's why you should give. It makes sense now that I'm an adult, and it's a lesson I pass on to my children, but as a kid, eating half a cookie was not filling at all!

So, if you have something to offer someone— your time, treasure or talents—remember you are doing pretty well for yourself, so don't hesitate to be generous toward others.

☼

Fire fast and hire slow.

Managers, listen up. You know how hard it is to fire someone if they're not working out—there are lots of HR processes involved and it could take a long time. The Davidism here is to encourage you never to rush to hire someone, even if they are the perfect candidate. Instead, take your time because that decision will last a while, and it needs to be well thought out.

Get a game plan in place on how and where you will look for an applicant, and then identify a set of peers to help you interview the candidate so you don't have a bias one way or another. This will provide you with a broader view of the applicant's personality, not just their technical capabilities. In short, develop a process to recruit and look for talent, and then a process to interview said talent, without taking any shortcuts. Now, when I say slow, I don't mean take a year to fill a position. What I do mean is to be more deliberate about the processes you follow—then take your time and actually follow them. So what if it takes an extra week to get the peer interviews done? It's time well spent that you won't regret.

The flip side of this Davidism is to fire fast. If someone isn't working out for whatever reason, move them out quickly. It doesn't matter if they've been there a week or five years—once you recognize the signs, and you've made an effort to find out if they're simply in a slump, don't hope and pray it will get better. Call HR and deal with it, NOW! If you don't, your team will see this lack of leadership and indecisiveness on your part, and their productivity will likely begin to slip, all because you're hesitant to take care of the deed. Even worse? In many cases, the slacker feeds off your weakness, knowing you're afraid to fire them, so they simply continue to "work" and get paid.

I realize this is probably one of the hardest things a manager has to do, but it comes with the role. If you can't handle it, get back on the assembly line.

Just

"I'm just an intern." "I'm just an executive assistant." "I'm just a receptionist."

Can you feel the low vibe of these statements?

I hope so!

Never use the word "just" to describe yourself—it minimizes who you are. In this context, the word means *simply*, *only*, *no more than*. So when you say I'm "just" an intern, or I'm "just" [fill in the blank], you are diminishing yourself. No one is "just" anything. You are a person with skills, abilities, feelings, views, and values, and there is nothing "just" about it.

☀

Ditch the "organizational chart" introduction.

Here's the scenario. You're at a networking event and someone comes over and introduces themselves to you. Your response is, "Hello, my name is Pat David. I work for Jane Doe." *Really?* That says nothing about you except who your boss is.

When you introduce yourself, don't introduce your boss. Instead, try something more intriguing that describes *you*, such as, "Hello, my name's Pat David. I'm the head of diversity, and I oversee the firm's diversity and inclusion strategy where we use data analytics to track and measure our progress to our plan."

Much better, right?

☀

Ladies: We don't want to hear you or smell you before we see you.

Yes, I'm talking about wearing noisy sandals or shoes and lots of perfume at work. You may not know it, but these things make you a distraction. Sure, this admonition raises gender stereotypes, but it's often the ladies who fall under this umbrella. So just remember: You worked hard to get where you are, and you expect to be taken seriously, so be mindful of how you are presenting yourself through others' eyes, nose, and ears.

Don't follow the herd, the herd gets slaughtered.

This Davidism is similar to the one I shared earlier about racing against yourself instead of against others, but this one urges you not to follow the crowd, the way people often do when they go in their parents' direction instead of their own. The wording of the Davidism is telling you to be more like the turkey that gets pardoned, or the lone steer or chicken that somehow escapes from the truck on the way to the slaughterhouse. In other words, be the one who gets to live their life out on a farm, in a zoo, or on some conservation site instead of on a plate for the family dinner.

I have always told my kids to follow their hearts and not to feel pressure to follow my path of Wall Street financial services, or my husband's route of the military—and I'll tell you the same. Find something you like that you are also good at. Because I worked on Wall Street and was part of the financial services community for many years, my kids might have been tempted to follow that path. In fact, many of the people I worked with or came across in that business pointed their kids in the same direction. Me? I never wanted my kids to feel directed toward any path that wasn't their own choice. I guess I did a good job of instilling this in them since both are in fields they enjoy—and a bit off the beaten path. As of this writing, my daughter is a herpetology keeper (she works with reptiles), and my son is an entrepreneur. They definitely did not follow the herd, and I am so proud they didn't.

☼

Kick yourself in the butt.

One of the most difficult things in managing one's career is figuring out ways to consistently stay motivated. You get into a routine of work, and the next thing you know time passes by and you've been in the same position for several years. The excitement you had when you first started is long gone. This is not a bad thing, per se, but if you want to move up and around, your lack of motivation can hinder your progress and affect your performance. Think about it: if your engagement is low, it will show in your work, how you interact with people, and so on.

How do you create that same level of excitement, engagement, and can-do attitude you had the first day you started working? Believe me, I know it's hard. It's like going to a Tony Robbins seminar and being energized by the crowd around you, all rallying for success, invoking good feelings just being among them. And then the event ends and you go back home. Although you may have had the time of your life, without Tony and those enthusiastic people, you cannot regain that same energy and excitement. It's the same thing with your job. The first day is nowhere near the 500th.

So, I want you to ask yourself: "What would I do if I could start over again?" Or, "If a person were going to replace me tomorrow, what are the one or two things I would tell them to do or work on?" Whatever you come up with, start doing it. This is one easy way to raise the bar and almost trick yourself into starting a new job in your current one by doing it in a new way.

I have actually tried this myself—I used to get bored quickly at work and was always looking for new ways to "trick" myself into doing my job differently or better. Reviewing all the ideas I had when I started my diversity role, for example, I would see which ones were still feasible, and then I'd start to implement them. It kept me motivated to redesign something, create a new dashboard, things like that.

Another thing you can do is to identify one or two things a year you want to improve on. Speaking in public, communicating for impact, learning pivot tables or macros in Excel, understanding how a function operates, the list goes on. My point is to identify an area, put together a plan of attack, and then attack! Gather a few people you trust in your professional circle and share your development goals with them. Get their support to keep an eye on you and help keep you on track. There is nothing more motivating than to have people sprinkled around in the organization watching you and rallying for you to improve.

Last, ask yourself what motivated you to take the job you're in now, and what are some of the things you haven't gotten to but still need to do? In other words, what would you work on if you had no barriers and would be able to start the job over with all the knowledge you now have—then get to work!

If you are serious about your career, this butt-kicking Davidism might just be the prescription you need. It does take practice to reinvent enthusiasm that has waned, but it can be done!

:☐:

Plan the work then work the plan.

When I was in college we had career day, when people with careers would file into the auditorium and share what they did, the skills needed for their jobs, the average salary one could expect, the type of projects they worked on, etc. During the one I attended, I raised my hand during the Q&A and asked, "What is the most important piece of advice you can offer us as college students?" I waited for something profound, something off-the-chart WOW, and instead I got, "Have a plan." *That's it?* I thought. *All you can say is "Have a plan"?* I was disappointed with her answer until she elaborated a bit more.

"As students," she said, "your days are pretty much planned for you. You choose your classes from the registration booklet, they're scheduled at certain times and days, and you have little choice on what time you have free. The twelve years from kindergarten to college were pretty much the same. So, as individuals, you didn't have to really think about your future—and that part of your brain was pretty much dormant or not working to the fullest."

Hmmm. Now she was making sense. Of all the advice I have ever received, this moved to the top of the list. *Have a plan.*

I had one more year to go in college, and then what? I realized then that "Have a plan" was great but needed a counterpart: "Work the plan." Why? Because it's not enough to have a plan; on its own it's just words on a page. But *working the plan* allows you to move from conception to implementation to completion.

So yes, have a plan, but you need to figure out how you're going to actually *work* that plan to bring it to fruition. Hone and direct your activities toward implementing and completing your plan. Be relentless with your time. Your calendar reveals where you spend your time so make it count. *Plan the work then work the plan.*

Would you hire you?

In the middle of my career, a senior person was giving advice to an audience of professionals. "Would you hire you?" he asked. After letting us chew on that for a bit, he said, "It's imperative that you maintain a critical distance to your own performance." Whoa. This made a huge impact on me.

Let's face it: this is one of the hardest things a person needs to do to improve themselves—taking a critical look and admitting to themselves they are average or need development. But trust me when I say it will change the way you work—and likely advance.

So, take a step back and think about how you do what you do. Really think about it. Are you always 100 percent or just sometimes great? Are you fully engaged in the work, the team, and the firm, or are you only partially engaged? If I observed you for a month, would I pick you out as the highest performing individual on the team? If you were building a high-performing team, would you be your first choice? Are you operating at rock-star status, or are you just a rock?

Before you answer, look at yourself from an outside perspective. The more critical you are, the higher your bar will be, and the harder or smarter you'll work to be at the top of your game—because no matter how good you are, you are always being measured against others—and if those people have a higher bar for themselves, are fully engaged, and are operating at rock-star status every day and under every condition, you will always be ranked somewhere underneath. But guess what? Even though this is true, the most important thing to remember is that you do your absolute best. Yes, there are a lot of variables involved in getting a raise or promotion, but asking yourself these critical questions is foundational for being the best you can be.

Once you have identified where you want to improve, go a step further: have a conversation with your boss and let him/her know you'd like to include them in your development plan. Say, "I've been doing my own self-assessment with a more critical eye toward my development, and I think in order to operate at the highest level, there are several areas I've identified I want to improve in. Here are some things I could use your help with . . . what are your thoughts?"

If you've never done this before, you may have to scrape your boss off the floor. But one thing is for sure: it will be a great conversation. When your boss becomes a partner in your development, they will not only be more aware of your commitment, they'll be more apt to see improvement in you because they know what to look for.

So, start your day tomorrow with this Davidism and ask yourself, "Would I hire me?" The answer should always be yes. If it's not, please reread this section.

:◌:

It's your performance review – own it.

Here's the deal in brief: Never leave a performance review without getting specific feedback on what you can do to improve. Even if your boss says you're doing a good job and to just keep doing what you're doing, you need to be prepared with your own questions ahead of time.

The reason for this is because it will a) let your boss know you've given thought to your own performance, which is admirable; b) show your boss you're in partnership with him/her; c) demonstrate that you are serious about developing yourself; and d) show you are open to receiving honest feedback. When you present ideas of where you think you can improve, it gives your boss the opportunity to add more areas of development, so be sure when you go in that you're ready to welcome those suggestions with open arms.

How about if your manager asks *you* to document your performance, and he/she will review it and make additions or comments? Embrace the opportunity! This is one of the few times you will be in 100 percent control of documenting not just *what* you did, but the breadth, depth, and scope of it. If you leave it up to your boss to do this, he/she will likely shortcut it, writing down the *what* but not the *how*. So see this as a chance for you to highlight your value instead of leaving it up to your boss.

I want to emphasize here that you never want to have a development conversation with your boss and have it turn into an argument. It should be a respectful discussion between you where you listen and ask questions, not try to wrestle your opinion to the ground. Many famous senior leaders call feedback a gift—accept it with grace and humility, then use it.

Here's how I want you to enter every performance review:

1. Do some self-reflection and write down areas you want to improve (even star athletes are always raising their game).

2. Speak with your boss in a partnership way as opposed to in an employee-boss way.

3. Show genuine interest in your growth and improvement, and in your boss's guidance for doing so.

4. If these tactics fail to work with your particular boss for some reason, as they say in Brooklyn, "Fuggetaboutit!" Either do your best to improve the targeted areas on your own, hope you get a more engaged boss in the near future, or start looking for a new job (though that's no guarantee of scoring a better boss!).

Walk with a purpose.

I joke with my team about a technique I use when I'm interviewing someone. I walk with them to my office, and if they are several steps behind me, their fate has been sealed. *wink*

Okay, I'm not that hard core. But I do think that when a person walks like they have somewhere to go, they make a strong impression. Call it smoke and mirrors, but I walk as if I actually have somewhere to go, and I often hear people say, "Pat is going places."

Think about it: when you see someone move quickly and head in a direction with purpose, you kind of assume that's part of their demeanor and personality. I did this all the time—even if I wasn't on my way somewhere. I'd walk like I was late for a meeting, and people thought I was so busy because I walked fast and with purpose (and of course I had the obligatory folders or reports under my arm!).

Sometimes it's a good idea to look the part—and I'll admit, I liked to walk fast because it was harder for people to stop and chat me up!

Wine is for drinking, so don't whine.

No further explanation necessary.

That's it for the appetizers and the warmup! Now let's get to some real-life questions I have been asked. Hopefully some of these will resonate with you and can help get you on your way.

What My Mind Was Thinking Versus What My Mouth Was Saying

You know how it is when you get asked for advice, when the person's question might make you want to internally roll your eyes, but you try to say something that won't make them feel bad for asking? Well, not to sound cold, but that happened to me at work *a lot*. People would often call, e-mail, stop by my office, or grab me in the hall and ask questions about their career, or simply seek advice or direction on something they were contemplating, and I'd have those moments of my mind having one answer (think: what you wish you could say but wouldn't be polite), and my mouth delivering another. With that in mind, I thought you might find it helpful (and at times, humorous) if I shared these dueling responses with you —not only for a few laughs, but for the insight you might gain from seeing both.

Here goes!

My manager doesn't give me career advice. What should I do?

🗨 **WHAT MY MIND WAS THINKING:** Go to someone else who will!

🗨 **WHAT MY MOUTH WAS SAYING:** Look, you should never assume your boss went to career-advice school and has an advanced degree in this area—especially if your boss hasn't moved in years. Believe it or not, this is one of the toughest requests a manager gets: giving career advice. Sure, you should be able to find someone who can offer sound guidance, but each individual should be able to chart their own career.

➤ **THE BOTTOM LINE:** Managers are very good at getting things done, such as projects, budgets, reporting, and the like, but when it comes to career advancement, this is where managers—and dare I say, companies— fall short. So, it's best if you don't rely on your boss as your one and only advisor, and instead have a number of people you trust that you can turn to for advice. Your HR department also has a good number of resources (they're not called Human Resources for nothing!).

Before you ask for career advice, though, always reflect on where you want to be and what you want to do. What goals or aspirations do you have? What skills are you good at, and what areas can use those skills? This way, when you do ask for advice, it's more structured and has some meat to it. In other words, don't approach someone with a blank slate. At the same time, if you are looking for someone to tell you what to do so that you can blame them if it doesn't work out, you better look in the mirror. No one is accountable for your actions except you. **Be your own catalyst for your career.**

I asked my manager for feedback on what I can do to get a promotion, and he/she said, "Just keep doing what you're doing." What does this mean?

WHAT MY MIND WAS THINKING: It means your boss has no development feedback for you and is taking the easy way out to get you off his/her back. It means they have no clue and are reciting classic rhetoric that has no meaning at all. It means they are kicking the can down the road and stalling you for another year. It may also mean you have reached the highest point and are not promotable. It means they are lazy, don't care, and hope you go away until next year. It may also mean they have no plan to promote you, so they will say something to hopefully pacify you and make you feel good so they can feel like they answered your question. The funny thing is, you just might let them get away with this classic yet shallow response.

WHAT MY MOUTH WAS SAYING: The problem is, you weren't clear. Asking for what you need to do to get a promotion is elusive at best, and there is no answer to that question. Unlike in the military or the police force where there are standards in place and clear requirements for upward succession, promotions to a corporate title aren't standard. Yes, there are rubrics and competencies and all of that, but even if you fulfill all of them, moving up doesn't happen automatically. Only a small number of people get promoted, even though many may by "eligible" and have the same tenure and performance.

➤ **THE BOTTOM LINE**: What makes some people more appealing to promote than others? Sometimes it's likability. Other times it's relationships or your level of engagement. All of these are factored into the equation.

Now, if you really want the truth, which may be hard to swallow, you need to be brave enough to be direct and say: "Let me ask you straight out . . . even with all the hard work I put in, and all I do to develop relationships, get my name out there, and show I'm a culture carrier . . . based upon what you know and have seen, is there anything about my character or persona that is a non-starter or that will always make me get voted down?"

The trick here is that you can't be angry with the

response if it is a yes. This answer signals that your likability factor is low, and I would therefore suggest you check out *The Likeability Factor: How to Boost Your L-Factor and Achieve Your Life's Dreams* by Tim Sanders. Yes, this is another one of life's hard lessons, but don't think of it as a reason to get down on yourself; think of it as an opportunity to grow.

Here are some concrete tips for having a conversation with a mentor or boss about your promotability:

* If you go the route of first doing a self-assessment, and you determine that based on the criteria for getting a promotion, you believe you have all of the competencies and have proven yourself consistently over the years, that's a good start.

* If your manager/mentor agrees, but *you* think there are a few things that may be holding you back, tell them you want their feedback.

* Ask if there are key relationships you need to foster so that when your name is mentioned in the promotion committee, more people know who you are and can speak on your behalf. Ask if there are any corporate culture–type of efforts you need to get involved in or be on a more visible project.

The point here is to give your boss ideas

up front on what else *you* think may be missing or what *you* may need to work on to improve your chances of getting promoted. This tactic opens the door for your boss to agree that these are development areas or to provide others— and it also makes your boss believe you are open to feedback because you took the lead and provided what may be showstoppers. This will also get the boss to partner with you on the "what's missing."

* If your boss says that in order to increase your chances for a promotion you need to develop relationships with senior people, you respond by saying, "That's great! Can we work together on making that happen?" Obviously, this is not a guarantee you will get promoted, but it's another sure-fire way to get your boss to be in partnership with you on what you may be lacking. It also helps your boss not to struggle with a response they may not want to discuss. Giving them ideas helps them get past this and allows them to be more open to tell you the truth on what is holding you back.

The Davidism in this one is to self-assess your growth needs, provide your boss with a baseline of development ideas, and, like it or not, understand the likability factor that might be hovering in the wings.

How do I ask for a raise? I don't think I'm getting paid fairly or what I think I'm worth. Maybe I need to leave.

WHAT MY MIND WAS THINKING: Getting paid fairly versus getting paid what you think you're worth is not the same thing. Don't even think of producing a thirty-page PowerPoint of what Glassdoor says you should get paid or detailing some analytical information you pulled off the internet. (Wouldn't it be funny if it showed you were getting paid too much—would you ask your boss to reduce your pay? I don't think so.) And whatever you do, don't calculate what your personal expenses are and ask for a raise to support your lifestyle. Your company's obligation is to compensate you a fair wage according to the market, not to pay your car loan.

WHAT MY MOUTH WAS SAYING: You don't need to leave to get a raise, but you *will* most likely get a raise if you leave. When a person changes jobs, it's not uncommon to get a 20 percent increase in pay. But if you're only leaving for the money, what you leave on the table are all of the non-cash—albeit valuable—assets, such as relationships you have forged, the professional equity you have established, and an appreciation for the culture of the organization.

Here is another thing to consider. Sometimes, when you do get that bump elsewhere, you may inadvertently be at the top of the range and will have to forgo any more increases thereafter. Because you will be at the top of that salary grade, you will probably want to leave that company a few years in to get another raise! And guess what? You now have to start all over again. So, if at all possible, I recommend you first try and work it out where you are.

➤ **THE BOTTOM LINE**: Always make asking for a raise a business proposition—don't compare yourself to others, and make sure you have clarity on your expectations. Make the conversation about you, your consistent performance—I repeat, *consistent* performance—your contribution, your future potential, things like that. Do NOT say, "I need you to give me a raise because I have bills to pay." This is not your boss/company's problem. But *do:*

* have an idea of what your expectation is (never ask for a specific dollar amount; ask for a percentage increase or a range instead)

* talk about your value to the team and your future potential

* ask your boss to identify several individuals

in comparable positions and do a review on
where you rank within that group

* possibly have your boss come back to you
with where you are comparable to others

Here is an example of how to approach a conversation with your boss on asking for a raise.

"[Boss's name], I'd like to sit down with you and
discuss my compensation. As you know, I've been
at the firm for XX years and have worked on a
variety of projects. I continue to excel in my job,
and I'm a culture carrier and strong team player. I
came into the firm at $$, and I realize I probably
should have negotiated a better starting point. As
of now, I think I'm off by [% or $$-$$] based
upon my performance, potential, and value to the
team. When I re-evaluate my compensation com-
pared to where I think it should be based on these
factors, I'd like you to review my history and my
future potential, and maybe after you've had a
chance to do that, we could discuss your views on
the matter. Thank you."

Another thing you need to know is what's called
"value of seat." A lot of companies participate in in-
dustry research to determine what the salary range is
for comparable-level positions in the same industry,
and they then use this research along with other fac-

tors to determine what they are willing to pay for a particular job. Depending on when you are in this "seat," the salary band could be wider or narrower.

It's important to keep this in mind if you ask for a raise because you think you're not paid to market. Why? Because your company likely has market intelligence to tell them what the salary range is for your comparable job. In most, if not all, cases a company will be able to say they are paying you within the range of the "value of seat" for that position. Now, you may be at the top end of the range for the seat you're in, but trust me, you are most likely within the range. This is why I recommend you find out from your boss or HR if the range is accurate. This way, you will at least know if a raise in the current seat is even feasible. Only *then* should you decide if you need to leave your company to get a raise.

Yes, this knowledge will at least put to rest your question about being paid fairly. But I have to be blunt and tell you that it almost doesn't matter what you think. The majority of people in most jobs fall within a salary grid. So unless you are at a high level and your value is critical to the future of the company, or you are a high-flying banker who knows how to make it rain (in which case you can almost certainly command a salary that is equivalent to what you believe you're worth), the value of what *you* are worth is probably on this grid. So if you want a raise, or better yet think you *deserve* a raise, the key to asking for one and getting one is not an exact science, but rather more of an art.

The Davidism here is to do some homework using the guidance I mentioned, and then take a step back and think about how you will present yourself appropriately to your boss.

I've been in this job for over five years, I work hard, and I'm still not getting promoted. What do I do?

WHAT MY MIND WAS THINKING: If you are repeatedly not moving up, you may have to join another race and hope your competition isn't as good as you. Oh! And there is no hard and fast rule that says you should move up after doing a job for two years, or even five years for that matter. Maybe you're just not as good as others in your position. Did you stop and think of that?

WHAT MY MOUTH WAS SAYING: Continue to work harder, but also work *smarter*—network, build more relationships, strive for more exposure. You also need to get clarity on your development plans and what you own to get promoted—and then act on it. Sometimes, even though you may be good, you may not be good *enough* compared to others in similar roles. That's simply because not everyone wins the race. So

I suggest working toward being the best at what *you* do. Strive to become the gold standard that all others are measured against. You will have a better chance of getting to the next level if you focus on your craft versus your title.

➤ **THE BOTTOM LINE**: Companies admire strong performers who are consistent over time—culture carriers who wear their corporate hat and think of the company first. Over the long run, operating this way will get you more points versus watching the clock for your next promotion.

Just like the "value of seat" point I raised earlier, companies sometimes perform an analysis and evaluate what's called the "span of control" at various management levels: how many direct reports, what levels/salaries are they at, that sort of thing. This exercise usually has an impact on the number of management levels, which has a direct impact on promotions and salaries. Organizations may, for example, increase the span of control for a manager, thereby eliminating duplicate or unnecessary management layers for cost savings measures. If this happens in your company, the outcome can definitely affect your ability to get an increase or a promotion. And, sad to say, I have seen instances where people were "right sized," meaning that their salaries were reduced to be more in line with the market research.

In spite of all this, however, your to-do list is still

the same. Continue focusing on your craft and being the best at it, and make sure your manager knows your desires and expectations, while keeping in mind that the variable is—and always will be—the other people you are being compared to for that promotion.

I get it. If you've been a role-model employee, worked the hours, completed the projects, done the requisite networking activities, and by all accounts performed your job as well as expected and are still not moving up, what gives?!

The Davidism here is that when it comes to promotions, although you have the performance, tenure, and/or competencies of what is required to get to the next level, *and* you can "check all the boxes," these are never guarantees the promotion will happen. Sometimes, even under all of these conditions, you will have to show proven consistent performance over time to even be considered to move up. And, truth be told, some companies will only put you up for a promotion at certain levels if they think you are promotable after that level. I also cannot stress enough that every time you're considered for a promotion, you will always be measured against a different group of people.

How do I find out what else I can do with my skills?

WHAT MY MIND WAS THINKING: What am I, a crystal ball? I just met you, so I don't even know what skills you have or what you are capable of.

WHAT MY MOUTH WAS SAYING: Always make sure your boss or team is well aware of other skills you have that you're not using. Your boss may have seen your resume when you got hired, but he or she doesn't carry it around with them. So, one easy way to bring your resume to life is to raise your hand to help out on something you have a skill in that is not part of your daily job responsibilities. People aren't mind readers, so always look for opportunities to share, demonstrate skills you're capable of, and offer experiences you had prior to joining the group.

Here's something I did quite often that may work for you. During a staff meeting, a one-on-one, or a team lunch, say, "I'm not sure if you're aware, but when I worked at [company name], I worked on a similar project. I actually have experience in [XX system or technology] / I know how to do [YY]."

Another can be to occasionally start a sentence by saying, "When I worked at [company name], we did something similar." Or, "In my last job, I was the lead on a similar project."

You can also show off your technical skills through your work. The next time you create a spreadsheet, for example, add a macro or pivot table, or add a feature (like a search field) that will make it easier for the recipient to use the file.

This kind of proactive approach is exactly how I became the chief of staff for the chief information officer (CIO), who was my boss. He wasn't particularly skilled at updating town hall presentations, and one day he stopped by my office and asked if I knew how to use PowerPoint. "Of course," I said. So he sent the presentation to me, and I used it as an opportunity not just to type what he said and make his presentation look great, but to also share my opinions and ideas on what I thought he should say. Before I knew it, he not only realized I could help him do more of these kinds of presentations, but he became acutely aware that I was likeminded and that I knew more than he gave me credit for. Prior to this, with me being head of technology for financial systems, my focus when I spoke to him was centered on the applications I was responsible for and the projects I had to deliver; there was never a reason for me to give him my views on his organization. But shortly after, he started to call me "Chiefy," which led to me being named his chief of staff—one of the best positions I ever had.

Had I limited my help to merely typing his dictation into a PowerPoint presentation, trust me, I would have never become his chief of staff. And the kicker was that this role gave me boundless insight, more responsibility, and access to key people, setting the stage for me to get the head of diversity position, which became a centerpiece of my professional career.

➤ **THE BOTTOM LINE:** Try to weave in skills or experiences you're not using in your job into everyday conversations, and figure out ways to keep your resume alive. When you do this, people will start to consider you the go-to person for some or all of your hidden skills, and a position, project, or experience may just come your way.

For reasons you can guess, this Davidism is one of my favorites: Keep your resume alive all day, every day.

My boss declined my request for a flexible work arrangement, what should I do?

WHAT MY MIND WAS THINKING: DON'T EXPECT THE COMPANY TO CONTORT ITSELF TO FIT INTO YOUR LIFE! It's not about you.

WHAT MY MOUTH WAS SAYING: If you really need the flexibility you asked for and didn't get it approved, consider requesting it in another way. Make it about the benefit to the *boss* instead of the benefit to *you*. Remember, you're in a job where things have to get done under certain conditions, so because quality and service matter, be sure you articulate how these two things will continue if you're on a flexible work schedule. But don't think this can happen by rolling your work downhill for someone else to do. You want to do a thorough self-assessment of your work and make sure you have a clear view of how it will get done *and* how customers will get supported under the schedule you've requested. You should also include in your conversation that your schedule can be re-evaluated in three months or so to determine if it's working as planned. Oh! And keep in mind that it's perfectly appropriate for your pay to be prorated based upon your flex schedule.

➤ THE BOTTOM LINE: You cannot get angry if you are denied a flexible work schedule. As a manager, I know the boss can't say yes to everyone and still maintain the quality and service of the work, so be thoughtful and understanding. Being a boss and having a team on a flexible work schedule is challenging and needs to be well thought out, so the more you can address potential issues and give the boss clarity and comfort, the better the outcome. In other words, be flexible with your flexibility request!

If this is a vital arrangement and the option isn't feasible in your current company, move on and find a position that's a better match. This is much more favorable than hoping for it to happen and wasting valuable time. Best to spend that energy finding a more suitable environment where you can have the balance you need.

I know this Davidism may be a little harsh, but it's called Be Realistic. The company hired you to perform a role at a fair wage. The quality of the product, the service to the customer, and the team performance and dynamics are expected to be held to a certain standard, and your flexible work arrangement request cannot disturb that model.

I have two great job offers that are similar and pay the same. Which one should I choose?

WHAT MY MIND WAS THINKING: Ummm . . . you should have thought about this beforehand. When you apply to multiple jobs, always have your criteria laid out and ready to save yourself time and stress.

WHAT MY MOUTH WAS SAYING: There are several factors and questions you should think about and ask when choosing a position, especially if they're similar in pay, position, location, and the like:

1.   Culture and people: Can you be yourself? Do you feel like you can be you in the company and not have any distractions? Have you met enough people where you feel like you'll fit

right in? I always say the two things that distinguish similar companies is people and technology, so try to find out which firm is a better match for your style and which has the tools best suited to you.

2. Ask yourself: What is the worst part of the position and would I want to do that? Sometimes we can get enamored by the money and title but at the end of the day, those things wear off and we have to do the work. If the answer is no, then the position is a no.

3. Although both jobs are similar, the way they'll get done will be wildly different. The question is: How do you have to *do* the work? As I illustrated earlier in the book, you have to find out if the position is structured in such a way that it will or won't bring out the best in you. In my case, the minute they said "every Monday we do this, and every Friday we do that," I was out. Too structured for me.

   What is *your* ideal work structure? If you don't yet know the answer to this, go back to the Davidism on page 15 and review my tips.

4. Think about which position has a better chance of getting you your *next* position. Each job you take should be a stepping stone to the job you really want. So, ask yourself what you

would learn in each position, if you would develop a strong professional network, and if you
would gain the exposure you need for the next
position you want.

5. Which job would provide you with a skill set
that you'll need to get your dream job? Think
about what or whom you will have access to
that would be a major differentiator a few
years from now and would round out your resume.

➤ **THE BOTTOM LINE:** Once again, I want to remind you
to ask these three key questions:

"How does the work get done?"

"What is the routine of the department?"

"If I was on the team last month, what would I
have been working on and who would I have been
meeting with?"

The responses should give you more intel on what
the difference really is between the "similar" offers
you have. It's an easy way to peel back the onion and
will provide you with useful information to make an
educated decision a lot quicker.

A new person joined the team, and the manager seems to like him/her better than me. What should I do?

WHAT MY MIND WAS THINKING: Be more likable. Come back to me if the relationship affects your job or career, not your feelings. Stop being childish, and do the work you're getting paid to do. Next question.

WHAT MY MOUTH WAS SAYING: You don't get paid to be liked, but you do get paid to execute. So as long as you're doing the work you're getting paid to do, who cares if your boss likes the new person? It's more important that your boss likes your work, not YOU.

➤ **THE BOTTOM LINE:** I'm not saying to ignore this situation because unfortunately, if your manager favors a coworker of yours for whatever reason, they can unconsciously give that person more money, put them on a better project, or simply treat them better. But this is one of those things you really cannot change. You can't make your manager like them less (unless you are so bothered by this that you seek out information to show your boss that this is a bad person and therefore not as likable as they think, which is clearly schoolyard type of stuff and not appropriate in business). The best you can do is to focus on your work and not let the situation get you off your game. I have seen people try so hard to be more likable and appease the manager that it actually backfires—not only does the manager see through it, but performance typically begins to suffer.

I know this firsthand because I committed this exact faux pas myself.

I was working in the technology department when a new woman joined the team and instantly hit it off with my manager, who was also a woman. They had similar likes in food, music, places they traveled, and so on. They went to lunch together and visibly enjoyed each other's company. Me? I had worked for this person for a few years, was a strong performer, and made her look good, and I'd not once had lunch with her. So when "Missy" started on the team and they connected so well, it really bugged me. I caught myself spending a fair amount of time watching their every move, trying to figure out how I could be more likable. Worse, I wondered how I could sabotage "Missy" and show my manager she wasn't as likable as me. Eventually, I realized it was a waste of time and gave up this strategy. I decided to focus on my work product, which was what really mattered. So what if my boss liked someone more than me? When it was all said and done, that wasn't how I should measure my performance or progress, so I just let it go.

Sure, there will always be people who are more likable than you and vice versa. The Davidism is to focus on what you can *influence*, not what you are *concerned* about. You don't need to be liked, but you darn well need to be respected.

How do I find a mentor?

(Sadly, people come to me and ask this question more than the one that follows.)

WHAT MY MIND WAS THINKING: Mentors aren't lost, so they don't need to found. And for heaven's sake, don't look at me—my mentor card is full. How come no one ever asks how they can find someone to mentor? Be a giver not a taker.

WHAT MY MOUTH WAS SAYING: There's no phone book of mentors or app for that—mentors will find *you* through your work. Your work is your biggest differentiator; it's your calling card. Mentors will seek you out and naturally want to be part of your success by giving you feedback. When I look back on my career, there were people who gave me honest feedback, put me in front of the right people, and took the time to steer me in the right direction—but I never referred to them as mentors. We didn't meet every Friday at three for an update, for example, but they saw me as a good person who was a hard worker with a lot of potential and no drama—*and* they genuinely wanted to help me. What I gave back was being a great employee and teammate who always performed at a professional level and put the company first. The people I considered my "mentors" were attracted to my work, personality, and positive attitude, and they were more than happy to open doors for me, help me move along, and in some cases, push me through the door.

➤ **THE BOTTOM LINE:** When I think about people I am drawn to and want to mentor, they are people just doing their job, treating others with respect, and not bringing any drama or bad karma my way. I mentor them without labeling myself a mentor.

Think about it this way: if a person gives you unsolicited advice after a presentation, that is a gift—they are mentoring you from afar. If a person submits your name for an award or project, they are also mentoring you from afar by opening doors for you. As in my case, there were many people when I look back who opened doors for me, gave me a push, and offered genuine feedback for no other reason than wanting to help me in my career. I still had to perform, work hard, and keep my nose clean, but they made my journey a whole lot better.

The Davidism here is that a mentor typically finds you based upon your work, character, and performance, so always be and do your best—you never know when someone is looking.

How do I find a mentee?

WHAT MY MIND WAS THINKING: Awesome! This person is a giver not a taker. I want to help them because they want to help others.

WHAT MY MOUTH WAS SAYING: We should all be more aware of the people we interact with on a daily basis. There is probably someone behind you on the career line you can reach out to—someone you see every day. Maybe there's a summer intern who looks a bit lost, or a new person on the team who could use some guidance. Just be more aware of the people you meet every day and the people you interact with, and I'm sure there's a person you can identify to help.

➤ **THE BOTTOM LINE:** Just like mentors are not in the phone book, neither are mentees. Don't wait for them to reach out because if they're looking for a mentor, they're lost and don't know where to find you.

When I think about all the people I have mentored and continue to mentor, in most cases it's not because they found me and asked me for help. It's where I may have noticed someone presenting and how they handled the Q&A, and I gave them unsolicited feedback because I wanted to help them be better. Or when I put a person's name up for a conference to help them expand their professional network, and so on. The point is, I reached out through normal activities in a business day. After giving people advice, I'd keep in touch with them along the way.

The Davidism here is to always be looking for someone to mentor. They are everywhere!

My boss is at the same level as me, and I was told I can't get promoted if he/she doesn't get promoted. What do I do?

WHAT MY MIND WAS THINKING: You know the answer: Get another boss.

WHAT MY MOUTH WAS SAYING: If what you're saying is true and you don't want to wait in that long line, then it's time to find another line. The choice is not, and cannot be, to expect the rules or guidelines to change for you. I'm sure you've already checked the organization chart to see how many people have the same title as their boss. There are many. You can either continue to whine about it and make some noise, or you can continue to work hard, expand your professional network, or look for a position internally or externally without these barriers that will slow down your progress.

⇗ **THE BOTTOM LINE:** This situation is not a unicorn and it is not an anomaly. Organizations are always trying to reduce costs and streamline management operations. Two very costly items in a company are management layers and title inflation—and companies prefer fewer layers of management in what I call the "belly of the beast," meaning where the majority of the labor gets done. This reduction helps speed up the decision-making process, but the kicker is that it also reduces opportunity for upward mobility and promotion.

If you find the perfect job and a great person to work for, you might want to ask if you and your boss are at the same level, and if that will have any bearing on you getting promoted in the future.

Remember also that "up" is not the only way. There is something to be said for moving laterally and acquiring broader skills. The key is to always look for roles where you are learning.

This Davidism is a tough one to swallow, I know. There will always be a number of stop gaps put in place for cost efficiency. They may be for all the right reasons from a business perspective, but they're not so good when it comes to you and your career.

Do I have to network with the people I work with?

WHAT MY MIND WAS THINKING: No, and guess what? They don't have to network with you either!

WHAT MY MOUTH WAS SAYING: No, you don't have to network with them, and you don't even have to like them (and they don't have to like you!). But you *do* have to work with them and develop relationships with them.

➤ **THE BOTTOM LINE**: You don't have to go out drinking and hanging out late with your coworkers, but you should know something about them and what they are about—and you should allow them to get to know you as well. As you develop a professional relationship with them, try to incorporate things about yourself during normal business activities, such as coffee breaks, lunch, walking down the hall, riding the elevator, or even at the beginning of a meeting when people are gathering. Look for moments of opportunity to get to know people and share who you are with them. All of these activities are considered networking.

The Davidism is simple: Don't get turned off by the word *networking*. Replace that word with the phrase "getting to know the people you work with and allowing them to get to know you."

How much of my personal life should I share with my team?

WHAT MY MIND WAS THINKING: Don't convert your

office to your living room with photos of your entire life. That's a bit much.

WHAT MY MOUTH WAS SAYING: You can share whatever you want, but understand the ramifications or risks of sharing too much. And if you're on social media, you've already shared a lot without even knowing it. A CEO once said that a book on you has already been written; anything I want to know about you I can find on social media—your personal life, your likes and dislikes, the sports teams you follow, your political views, the friends you keep. In other words, your personal life is likely already exposed, so if you're concerned about sharing too much of it, check your social media to see if it is in line with your concerns.

➤ **THE BOTTOM LINE**: My philosophy has been to share things with coworkers that are meaningful and would provide some connection to the business objectives of the group. For example, you can share a professional network you belong to, a second language you speak, or prior projects you worked on. A sample sentence you can use would be, "I'm not sure you're aware that when I worked at [company name] I was on [project name] and had to solve a problem similar to [fill in the blank]."

Another example is when I was asked to develop

a veterans strategy. In that case, I shared that my siblings were in the Air Force and my husband was a former Marine. This gave me credibility with the veteran community and was meaningful information to do the work.

In short, ask yourself: Is the information I'm going to share meaningful to the function, the problem we are trying to solve, or the project?

Now, if you want to share things about your kids, pets, or vacation plans, that's all well and good, but strive for balance without being a completely open book. For example, I recommend the strategy of following what people share versus sharing and hoping people follow. What I mean by this is, if a person tells you they have three children, you can respond with how many children you have. What you should *not* do is offer how many children you have, followed by their ages, names, hobbies, mannerisms, allergies, and that sort of thing. If you always respond equal to the other person's response, you cannot be accused of sharing too much, and you are keeping things balanced.

This Davidism reminds you to always think about *relevance*—connecting what you're going to share to how it can be applicable to business, whether it's a problem, a project, or simply appropriately expanding your relationship with those you work with.

My boss doesn't give Es (excellent/the highest performance review level). What should I do?

WHAT MY MIND WAS THINKING: That's great! You don't want them to *give* you an E, you want to *earn* an E. You're not in school anymore, so don't equate this to getting a varsity letter.

WHAT MY MOUTH WAS SAYING: If you commit to doing your absolute best every day you come into work, don't let the E thing get you off your game.

➤ **THE BOTTOM LINE**: This is one of those management perspectives you can disagree with, question, or even hate, but you may not be able to change your boss's position on this one. Sure, you can complain to HR, to other people, to your friends and family, but in the end nothing will change. You may have helped the department complete a critical project, picked up more work when someone left the team, ensured everything ran smoothly, and made your boss look good, yet still only achieved below an E. I know it stings, and the injustice of it *is* mind boggling, I agree. How can self-respecting companies allow this to happen? How is it acceptable for a manager to outright tell you that no matter what you do or how hard you work, you cannot earn the highest level rating? What will your motivation be to work hard? Why bother?

These are all valid questions. And my answer for you is: You make the efforts you do to reflect your brand—not to receive a particular "grade" for doing it. The gratification should be in what you give that is authentically *you*.

Look, I get it. We all like to be recognized in tangible ways for our hard work. I wish I had a better answer for this one, but I can only offer this Davidism: Always do your best for *you*, not for the "grade" or for what you perceive as the reward for doing it.

I achieved all of my objectives and my manager still didn't promote me or give me an outstanding review.

WHAT MY MIND WAS THINKING: All too often people think that just because they complete their objectives in a given year and check off all the boxes, they should get an outstanding review and a sack of cash.

WHAT MY MOUTH WAS SAYING: Although you may have completed all your objectives in a particular year, there are plenty of things that could come into play: you may not have set the right pace, you may have left a firestorm behind you, the company may have had a bad year . . . the list goes on.

➤ **THE BOTTOM LINE**: Remember when you were in school and the professor would share not only what your learning objectives were but also put a time-frame (a quarter or semester, usually) on it? The professor set the pace, right? But when you work in a company, you aren't told outright when you are supposed to learn something. You might assume you have your first year on the job to learn something, but because you never asked, you get surprised at the end of the year by a less than favorable review about how long it's taken you to pick up on a particular skill or task. This is why I implore you to *always* ask your boss not only what your objectives are but what your pace should be. Trust me, it will create clarity and make all the difference.

Another point here is that it's not just about getting the work done but how you *did* the work. Did you intimidate people or were you a good team player? Were you respectful and collaborative or a pain to work with? Remember, *doing* the work is important, but *how* you do it holds a lot of weight. A consistently high performance level is critical to getting promoted.

I know this topic comes up over and over again. Promotions are tricky because on paper you may have met all of the competencies, performance criteria, team expectations, and other specifics. But there are always a handful of variables. Who else will you be put up against in that promotion year? What are the other rules or guidelines that can affect your promotion? Who is on the promotion committee and would all of those individuals be supportive? Do those individuals know you? Yes, promotions at a certain level in an organization can be done at the manager level (for example, in investment banking). But once you get to VP and above, many others will be part of the approval process, and that's where the game changes. This is where relationships and exposure will matter a lot more than merely performance and checking off your objectives in any given year.

If you want to get to the next level, this Davidism is critical. Get your name out there and develop relationships with the right people. You don't want to be the name that comes up during the promotion committee meeting and a few people say, "If this person is that good, how come I don't know her?"

I have my masters degree, got great grades in school, and I'm not able to get a job. What am I doing wrong?

WHAT MY MIND WAS THINKING: School is over, and tests and grades don't matter. What *does* matter is the employment opportunities in your field, what your requirements are for work (a certain location, a flex position, a specific salary range, etc.), and oh yeah . . . don't forget about the thousands of other people who have a masters or a doctorate who are looking for jobs too. It's called competition.

WHAT MY MOUTH WAS SAYING: One of the keys to getting a job is casting a wide net, having relationships that have been fostered over time and skills that are needed. Don't become despondent or complacent; getting a job is a job in itself and you need to work at it every day. One of the easy things to do is to reach out to your professors—they don't just know things, they also know people in various industries. They can be a great resource to help you make connections.

➤ **THE BOTTOM LINE**: Try to interview for positions that wouldn't necessarily be your first choice—but that you *would* be willing to accept—in order to create a safety net. I'm sure you did the same when you applied to colleges—you had a few desired schools and a few "safe" ones. If you get an offer, even if it's not your top option, that's awesome! It shows you interview well, that you were poised, and that you came across professionally. Feel good that someone wants you *and* that you gained interview experience!

I also recommend that you think outside the box. What skills and capabilities do you have? Do some homework on what jobs match your profile—and don't assume you already know what those jobs are. Putting your resume on websites like Indeed can help because they look for keywords in your resume and present you with jobs that match your profile. There are thousands of jobs out there you've never heard of, as well as industries that aren't even on your mental checklist. Even if these jobs don't interest you, check them out and become smarter about what's available. You never know what that new knowledge could lead to.

Keep in mind that your resume should always include not just *what* you did, but *how* you did it. How complicated was the job? Was it global? Did you have to coordinate with multiple entities to do the work? This will help the recruiter or hiring manager understand the extreme conditions under which you had to perform specific tasks, and this could be the determining factor between you and someone else getting an interview.

My Davidism here is to remember that when presenting yourself, always include the breadth, depth, and scope of your work. You never know what will grab a potential employer.

Whew! There you have it: what my mouth was saying versus what my mind was thinking in response to real questions people have asked me over the years. I could have listed double what I shared here, but these were the ones I was asked the most. Dare I say that I bet you or someone you know has experienced many of these scenarios and maybe didn't handle them as well as you could have. Well, perhaps with these Davidisms under your belt, you can be better prepared if a similar scenario happens again.

EZ-Pass Davidisms for Early-Career Professionals

Perhaps you just graduated from college and are ready to find that perfect job. You have a good GPA and your resume is sprinkled with great internships, leadership experiences, and volunteer activities. You are ready to begin your search and have high hopes to make something of yourself. The objective on your resume reads:

> Highly motivated college graduate with internship experience. Seeking to leverage my acquired academic knowledge and work experience in a growing company. A dedicated worker, aiming to join a diverse team, where I can help solve complex business problems while I continue to learn and grow.
>
> (Feel free to plagiarize this for your resume if you like.)

Or maybe you have been out of school for a few years and are already working in a professional capacity. You have a good job, you've been doing your part to learn, you like the people and the feeling is mutual. You might also be a great team player who is both growing in your craft and active in company events. With your strong reviews, you have high hopes to make something of yourself, but you're starting to wonder how you can progress—and how much time it might take to do so.

You may also be someone who has been in a professional environment for several years and for some reason are in a rut. The excitement has worn out, your promotions have stalled, your network consists of your family and friends, and you don't have a positive outlook on your trajectory. You think you are doing everything right but feel alone and don't have a trusted place to turn for advice or guidance. You might even be thinking of quitting in exchange for a position where you will be happier and better cared for.

If you fall into one of these categories, don't fret —you are still early enough in your career where we can make some Davidism adjustments. There are a number of habits you can start doing now that will help strengthen your base with respect to your career and kick it back into action.

What I have observed is that everyone at these levels spends a fair amount of time focusing on the functional and technical skills necessary to do their jobs. They work the hours and put in the time; they do everything right (at least based on what they have been told). Basically, they heed the advice my mom gave me when I was just starting out (do your job, go to work earlier than the boss, leave after the boss, and keep your nose clean). Obviously, there is nothing wrong with operating your career this way, because if you are getting paid to do the work, you better know how to do it well, right?

Unfortunately, this is not a career plan; this is a "go to work and don't lose your job" plan. Sure, it will put you on the assembly line where you get your requisite annual increase and, maybe if you're lucky, a promotion in three to five years. And if you're super lucky, you could even get to manage a team. But if you want to be successful, this is not the plan that will move you up the ladder. You may succeed but not excel. To excel and really go further and faster, there are some soft skills and behaviors that you need to develop.

No matter which timeframe you fall into, there are a handful of things I have observed from people at every career stage that have made the difference in achieving success sooner rather than later—hence, this list of EZ-Pass Davidisms for early-career professionals.

(To be honest, I can't figure out why some people don't buy the EZ-Pass. How many times have you crossed a bridge and waited in the long line to pay the cash toll while the EZ-pass folks drove right through?) In any event, let's get back to you.

I came up with the habits below so you could develop an advantage and stop waiting on line with the poor saps who don't have EZ-Passes.

Build internal networks – at multiple levels.

You have heard a million times that your network determines your net worth—and it's actually true. The network I was able to build early in my career is the reason why I'm financially stable today. My network, especially my professional network, helped me excel and succeed faster and further than I would have if I had gone it alone. But it's not enough to solely have this network. The real lesson, or Davidism, here is to understand there are *multiple types of networks*, each of which needs to be refreshed over time as you grow.

Here are six informal networks you should always have as you mature in life. Think of these as basic ingredients, or staples, for a successful career.

The first network most people have early in life is their *Friendship / Social Network.* The people in this network are the ones you have fun with, likely grew up with, and maybe even went to school with. These are the friends who generally have similar interests and are the ones you can call anytime to give you a ride or loan you some cash.

Your Friendship/Social Network also has many other "friends," those you are connected with on social media, who may or may not be actual friends. I emphasize this because this network allows people to share ideas behind a computer screen, and as such can be the one that causes you the most grief if you're not careful about how you use it and present yourself to the world. This is also the one network that is the most vital to review and upgrade over time. The social networks you had in high school or college might have been fun to be part of, but as you begin to develop your brand, be very careful—those networks will define you. It's called "guilt by association," and your prospective employer will have all your activity at their fingertips when they do a background check. So please, be mindful of the networks you keep and the networks who keep *you*.

I Google myself every now and then, just to find out who I am to the public. As expected, there is a lot of information about my professional career from my time at JPMorgan chase as head of diversity, as well as various interviews I've done and awards I've received, all of which are favorable (thank goodness!). But the rude awakening for me was the first time I Googled myself and clicked on *images*. Wow! There sure were a lot of photos of me throughout the years. The big lesson for me was: I NEED A MAKEOVER.

As I write this book, I am wearing the same earrings and have the same necklace and hairstyle I did when I got my doctorate in 2016. Yikes. And yes, I still have the suit I wore when I received the Patricia

David Trailblazer award. And let's not forget that red jacket I was photographed in during the 90s (that's 1990s, not *1890s*).

Sad, right? But at least they all still fit. Anyhow, back to you. Do yourself a favor and Google yourself.

When I said you have to refresh your networks over time as you grow, note that this includes refreshing your friends too. You have to distinguish which friends you will have serious career conversations with versus which ones you will party with, or which friends you will keep and which ones you won't. The fact is, not all of them will be in line with your journey and progress at the same pace as you, and it's okay if certain friendships drift apart or simply end because the time has come for you to go your separate ways.

The second type of network, which most people think of when discussing business and career, is your *Professional Network*. These include people you develop relationships with in business over time. Now, let's be clear: this is not you collecting business cards from everyone you meet and stacking them up as high as you can so you can boast about your professional network. I'm talking about people you connect with often (not every Friday at 3:00, but often enough). These people share a professional connection with you, are like-minded, and share mutual respect. These are people you reach out to when you need advice or direction on anything from getting a new position to moving to another area or dealing with a certain manager. This network can include people at all levels and come from varied backgrounds. As you grow in your career, you carry these individuals with you. I still interact with and reach out to my first manager, sometimes just for a quick hello, or when I need advice on an opportunity I'd like her thoughts on. The point is to keep these relationships fresh and current.

The third is your *Emotional Network*. This network includes people from work, your community, your school, your family, or whomever you can reach out to for emotional support—such as when you lose a loved one and need someone you respect to help you through your emotions, or when you feel gut-punched because you didn't get that promotion, or are on the verge of going crazy at work and need to just scream or cry. These are the people with whom you are comfortable discussing your feelings, the ones who won't judge you and will listen with their heart not just their ears, and who will help you get your mojo back.

Fourth is your *Ethical Network*. This is for the times you may end up in a situation where your ethics are tested and you need to speak with someone who is trustworthy and can help you weigh your options.

These are people in your network who are level-headed, honest, and have a strong moral compass. When your integrity is being compromised, this is your tribe for advice and counseling.

The fifth is your *Spiritual Network*. The people in this network don't have to be priests, rabbis, or other spiritual leaders, but they are people you can reach out to when you question your faith (whatever it is you believe in). After I lost my dad, sister, and brother within a two-year period, I was ready to give up and say, *What's it all for?* I have a few friends who listened to me without judging, patronizing, or schooling me, and in doing so helped me get my faith back.

And sixth and final is your *Academic Network*. This is the group that includes professors, guidance counselors, or people in academic institutions who have seen you grow into an adult. Perhaps they took a special interest in you during your academic life, or showed kindness and caring toward you and offered advice. To this day, I regret not keeping in touch with any of my college professors; if I had, I probably would have gone to law school, which is what I really wanted to do. But because I wasn't smart about networking or asking for advice at the time, I never asked the big question: "How do I become a lawyer?" The even bigger tragedy was that I went to Fordham University, which has a law school. Duh!

You'll likely find that people in your network belong to one or more of these six groups. That's great! The point is that you need to have people you respect, and who respect you, to help you get through the varied challenges you encounter. Life can be hard at times, and it's not a rehearsal, so it's more than okay to have help along the way.

Another way to think about having these networks is on a more personal level. For example, if you needed to have some plumbing done, get your car serviced, or have yard work done, it's nice to able to say, "I've got a guy/gal for that." You probably have a guy or gal for any number of things you need help with for your house, apartment, or car, right? And as you live your life, you capture more of them as part of your personal network.

So think of this as you manage your career: You gotta get a guy or gal—because just like when things go wrong in your personal life, they may also go wrong in your professional life.

My goal is for you to be able to use some or all of these EZ-Pass Davidisms to learn from my past to develop your future.

For Starters

I recommend writing these on index cards or snapping a photo of them with your phone and reading them every morning to get ready for your awesome day.

* Be clear how you define success at every step of your career, and also how you define it with your boss.

* Know when to sweat the details and when to take a step back and see the big picture.

* Don't be impatient with your career, but make sure you are ready when the next opportunity arises.

* Proofread your emails before you send them, and ask yourself if you'd be proud or embarrassed if your mom read them.

* Stay informed. Your clients expect it, so always know what matters to them.

* Enjoy a healthy dose of competition—it will make you better.

* Never get relaxed if/when you think you have won. Someone is always out there trying to one-up you.

* Don't be too risk-averse—if you avoid risk, you won't be challenged enough.

* Learn from your mistakes and move on.

* Listen to learn, not to respond.

* Continue to be a life-long learner in order to remain relevant.

* Always take advantage of whatever experiences, resources, and opportunities you are given.

Can I, Will I, Do I

When I think about my career and all the business-people I encountered, I reminisce about how fortunate I was to work with and get to know quite a number of successful individuals. Always curious about how they became successful, I asked many of them to tell me their stories—and their secrets. Much of what I heard was categorized as "unwritten rules," so I decided to write them down, thinking, *why would anyone keep these a secret?*

My idea was to create a tool or cheatsheet for people to carry with them, something easy to understand that they could apply to themselves—and that would be timeless. In fact, I created these Davidisms about two decades ago and they are still relevant today.

What surprised me was when I looked back on my own journey and how I became successful, I discovered I used many, if not all, of these in some shape or form. However, none of them were planned; they either simply happened, or I was just lucky. In other words, early in my career, none of them were what I would call deliberate. But as I learned more and became more aware of how to manage my career, I was increasingly relentless with myself in making these actions habitual.

My mom always said, "You get out of something what you put into it." I hope that wherever you are on your journey, you take charge of your career right now and be relentless with it. After all, it's yours. I highly recommend you go to my website at www.patricia-david.com/I-Can and print the PDF of the following "I CAN" statements as a reference to carry with you. You can even frame it in your office or make it your screensaver or background on your phone. This way it will always, and I mean always, be with you. Ultimately, you want to develop these as *habits*—acquired behavior patterns regularly followed until they become almost involuntary. (One of my good habits is that I always return a phone call. One of my bad habits is I will eat the entire bag of Lays family-size potato chips while my family isn't watching!)

I can understand what type of environment increases my productivity.

When I worked at Burger King, I had to make burgers and nothing else. You already know that the assembly-line operation was decidedly *not* for me, even though I made burgers faster than anyone on our team. Roll the clock forward to working in more professional organizations where I would have to take on key projects, or build mega complex systems. For some people, this would be stressful, but I was always jazzed. "The gnarlier, the better" suited me perfectly. I would get excited to think about how I was going to fix something because to me, that was the challenge that made every day different, where I was able to use my creativity and always be thinking of solutions. So, whenever I was considering a new position, the first thing I wanted to know was how similar to BK it would be. If it was too organized and structured with little to no creativity, I would pass, knowing it wouldn't be the environment that would make the best of me come out. I urge you to know this about yourself and do the same.

I can be honest about my limitations, what I'm good at, and what I enjoy.

When we are asked to do a self-assessment or self-evaluation, we sometimes tell ourselves little lies. But it's vital to know where your strengths lie, as well as what you honestly excel in and like to do. For me, anything that requires speaking and influencing, my hand goes up; the minute someone talks about preparing detailed work papers (for an update with a level of detail not even seen by the military), I am like a church mouse. Know what makes your hand fly up and what makes you clam up. It will serve you well in what you do.

I can speak to someone I trust who can help make my dreams come true.

Let's say you have an idea you feel strongly about that you want the firm to get behind. If you tell this to a colleague or peer, three things can happen: one, they can steal your idea and get to your boss first; two, they can make fun of it; or three, they can sabotage it. Even expressing you would like a new opportunity or to try something in a new area, to anyone other than a person who can help you achieve it, is merely chitchat. The person who needs to hear this is your boss. Why? Because they're the one who can make it happen.

Now, I know that in some cases, a person doesn't trust or feel comfortable speaking to their boss about their dreams. But sometimes the opportunity will present itself. My boss once asked me during a review what else I wanted to do, and I replied I'd like to be the head of diversity, head of communications, or a function that dealt more directly with people (I share the full story of what came from that pronouncement on page 128). He was the only one who could make any of these choices happen—and I put my trust in him. Had I shared my aspirations with my peers, it's quite possible their name would have ended up on the slate instead of mine. So, be mindful of who you share your aspirations with, and seek a mentor or boss you can trust to hear them.

I can do some research on what opportunities are available.

Don't be like that person who plops down in a person's office and says, "What else can I do with my skills?" Or, "What opportunities are available out there?" Do your homework and come prepared with information, *if* you want to get help. It shows you are invested and not just being lazy. It's not only disrespectful, it's not fair to rely on other people to direct you, so demonstrate that you've done your own legwork.

I can network, get to know people outside of my current job responsibilities, and build strong relationships with senior management and other people of influence.

This speaks to the point I raised earlier in the book: constantly build your networks, whether they be social, academic, ethical, professional, or others. Remember, the more people you know, the more people know you.

I can continue to educate myself and stay current in my area of expertise, and take advantage of internal and external learning opportunities.

In order to be relevant, you need to keep up with your craft and be valuable to the organization. In short, if you're not willing to be a continuous learner, you will be obsolete real quick. You need to keep your mind fresh. Read, and read some more. If you have an opportunity, join a professional organization. Subscribe to newsletters. Attend conferences where you can learn about new trends in your craft and network with like-minded people. I was always reading research and surveying material about diversity and inclusion, or technology and new regulations, in the workplace. I was able to attend conferences and even spoke at many. This was my way of remaining relevant. So keep in mind that our company, our clients, and our staff expect us to be on the forefront of knowledge. It's therefore important to stay relevant with respect to your competence.

I can take ownership of my career.

You already know this but it bears repeating: It's *your* career, not your boss's or your company's. And if it is important to you, why would you give it to anyone else to maintain and manage? Remember what my mom said: "You get out of something what you put into it."

I can be a mentor to others.

No matter where you are on your journey, even if you're just starting out, there is always someone behind you. So look back, reach out, and help pull someone up (and buy them a copy of this book—they, and I, will appreciate it!).

Why do all of these statements begin with "I can"? Because giving up *is* not, and *should* not, be an option. There is nothing you can't do if you truly want to do it.

My

What follows are seven categories that can help provide a compass in knowing if you're suited to a particular job by asking a handful of simple questions.

MY COMPANY

Do I believe in the company?

Do I believe the values of this company are in line with my own?

Do I believe that the company is well led?

MY BUSINESS

Do I believe that there is a sustainable competitive advantage?

Is the business I will be working in profitable?

Is there a sustainable business model?

MY COMPENSATION

Will I be paid fairly for what I do?

Will my performance be evaluated against set goals and objectives?

Will superior performance be recognized?

MY MANAGER

Do I know what is expected of me?

Will my manager give me feedback?

Will my manager care about my development?

Will my manager recognize my performance?

Will my manager be open to ideas?

Will I be treated fairly?

MY DEVELOPMENT

Can I learn here?

Can I have growth experiences here?

Can I advance my career here?

Will I do interesting work?

MY COLLEAGUES

Will I work with good people?

Will my colleagues be committed to quality work?

MY LIFE

Will I have a life?

Will I make time to laugh and be happy despite working hard?

Will I be able to be me and bring my whole self to work?

None of these has a right or a wrong answer. But if you are wondering or deciding on how to choose to stay with a company or to work for a new one, or if you're thinking of what questions to ask based upon where you are in your career or even during a job interview, these Do I's, Can I's, and Will I's will help provide you with structure to determine the right answer for *you*.

A Mentor, a Sponsor/Advocate, a Coach, and a Mole

I know, this sounds like the beginning of a "walked into a bar" joke. But these four entities are actually vital components of your career, and I'm going to break each one down for you so there's no confusion because frankly, when I began my career, I was totally clueless. In fact, the only reason I am able to provide Davidisms on this topic now is because in addition to three decades of working in corporate America at an executive level, I was also fortunate to head up a diversity practice at Citigroup and JPMorgan Chase. Working in this field gave me access to information that most people wouldn't have, and it also provided me with a lot of research, surveys, and intelligence about the key ingredients to a successful career. I read a lot and learned a lot, most of which I would have liked to know thirty years prior—which is why I want to explain the differences between these roles, when you need them, and how important it is to renew and review people who take on these roles in your support system, hopefully when you're still early in your career.

One of the things I never realized years ago is that as your life and career goals change, your support system needs to change with it. Also, you could probably get away with one person playing each of the four roles in this chapter, but I would suggest against it. In my opinion, it's better when you have a clear demarcation for the person to be effective in steering you and giving you advice. This is because when you're meeting with your mentor, the circumstances can be wildly different from when you're meeting with your coach, and so on. Read on and you'll see what I mean.

What is a mentor for?

MENTORS SPEAK <u>WITH</u> YOU.

As you begin your career, you want to find people you have a genuine connection with on a professional level, who have similar interests, and who you admire, trust, and can have an honest conversation with— people who have some measure of success and are balanced thinkers with a high level of integrity. (As previously noted, don't go up to someone and ask them to be your mentor—this is the kiss of death and a non-starter for a relationship. Let mentors find *you*.) Mentors not only are good listeners, have empathy for your story, and provide general guidance and direction, but they are concerned about your overall progress and trajectory and are there to help guide you to reach your aspirations.

Keep in mind that the mentor/mentee relationship is a two-way street. Your conversations shouldn't always be about you; check in on your mentor as well. As they inquire about what they can do for you, ask how they are doing and see if you can offer any assistance to them too. In other words, don't just take from them, give something back. By doing this, you can also continue to gauge if this person is good for you over time.

Refreshing your support system is also easier if you keep in touch with your mentor. And while it might sound a little cold, though a mentor genuinely cares about you and is there to guide you, they are not necessarily your friend. Yes, a friendship can develop with time, but remember that their primary role is to give you guidance, not hang out with you.

Which brings me to the $64-million-dollar question: Where can you find these people? No, it's not through a website, an app, or a membership service. As I said earlier, the way you find a mentor is to work hard, maintain a high level of integrity, and be visible. Your performance, personality, and character will be your guide.

One of my longest standing mentors has guided me in multiple ways without me even asking him to take on this role. While I was in the technology field, this man was my client. Over time, as we built trust, he took genuine interest in me and started giving me general advice, which included everything from how I presented to how I spoke in public. One time he pulled me aside and told me I spoke too fast and should slow down. "Why is that a problem?" I asked. His response was, "You have so much good information to share, you need to slow down to make sure people hear what you have to say." Well, from that day forward, whenever I made a speech or presented, I inserted the word PAUSE in my notes. It forced me to slow down—and it worked. It was sound guidance I remember to this day.

As time went on, I made it a point to reach out to this mentor to see if there was anything I could do for him. A few times, I actually found myself mentoring *him* (unsolicited, of course!). We eventually became friends and to this day keep in touch with a mutual level of respect for each other. And to think the relationship started out by me simply doing my job as the head of technology for HR.

Just as my mentor reached out and gave me unsolicited advice, I hope you take some time to think of the people you come into contact with. Perhaps someone junior to you (family, coworker, acquaintance) can use some caring, unsolicited feedback and guidance. Remember: there is always someone behind you, so turn around and see who's back there.

What is a sponsor/advocate for?

SPONSORS/ADVOCATES SPEAK FOR YOU.

As you start moving up in your career, sponsors and advocates become more crucial. These people differ from mentors in that they likely have a line of sight to your work and see you in action in some way, know you from a distance, and/or hold you in high regard. Because they are influential and are connected to senior people, they have power and authority to make things happen; their broad networks can get you or your name into rooms or conversations just because people respect and listen to them. Think of a sponsor/advocate as someone who will make sure you're known by the right people. They are individuals who will open doors for you, raise their voice to nominate you for a promotion or award, and bang their hand on the table if people dare to defame your name or character.

Early in my career, I can honestly say that not knowing I needed an advocate or a sponsor probably lost me three to five years of progress because I was going it alone. The problem was, *I didn't know what I should have known.* Once senior people took an interest in me, however, things started to happen. I got nominated for awards, got promoted, and was invited to conferences and asked to join various committees. My sponsors and advocates put my name out there and it lifted me up.

You may be wondering where these people came from. At first, I didn't know who they were myself. What happened was that as I started to gain more exposure, I would ask how I made it on a certain list or who nominated me for a particular position or award, and names of senior people would be mentioned. When I contemplated why they chose me, I could think of only two things: my performance and my character. Yes, many of these people were distant in that I could not reach out to them like I could my mentor and check in. But they were willing to associate their names with mine, and as I became more familiar with who they were, I made triple sure I was operating at my highest level whenever they were around. I did this not just to shine in their presence, but because I knew their reputation was on the line, and I wanted to be sure I lived up to it.

I have also played the role of sponsor/advocate to scores of people. For example, if everyone was throwing out names of people to be considered for a top job, and I knew a person in my network had the correct credentials and would do well but their name wasn't being mentioned, I would vocalize that individual's name and make sure they got proper consideration. To be clear, I would only do this for people who had a high level of integrity and performance because, guess what? My name would be associated with them and I had to protect my personal brand. But if their only crime was that no one in the room knew them, it was my duty to give them exposure. In many cases these individuals didn't even know I was doing this. It was only when a few of them got a job or an opportunity they weren't actively pursuing and asked HR or the hiring manager how they landed on the list that they were told it was me.

So, if you get invited to a conference, or nominated for an award, or gain access to something out of the ordinary, ask who put your name on the list and I bet you'll find you have sponsors out there watching you. And if you are in a room and have a chance to sponsor or advocate for someone, don't hesitate to make your voice heard.

What is a coach for?

COACHES SPEAK TO YOU.

While mentors speak *with* you and sponsors/advocates speak *for* you, coaches mostly speak *to* you in a one-way conversation, either to help you improve your technique, heighten a particular function or skill, or learn something specific. This is a person who coaches you on what to say during an interview, or how to handle an issue with your manager, or how to swing a bat. They can also assist in developing skills such as communicating for impact or building your personal brand.

One of the people who played the role of my coach helped me prepare for my first of many board presentations. He gave me tips on how to perform, what to present, and what to expect. After listening to me do a dry run, he gave me tips and challenged me with potential questions I might get. (He was the one who planted the sage advice in my head: *Don't think every question needs to get answered.*) This man's coaching was invaluable to me; his role was critical to how I was able to carry myself at a senior level. But he was not my friend (at least not in the beginning). Yes, a coach can end up being a friend, but their primary role is to help you improve in a given area. Your role is to listen, absorb, and perform.

Unlike mentors and sponsors/advocates, coaches are easier to find. Some organizations provide senior-level people with coaches as part of their development plans, and these coaches usually come from or are coordinated through the HR department. So if coaching is something you think you need, speaking with HR is a good first step—but you must be specific about what you would like coaching on so the best match can be made for you.

You can also find a person to coach you by asking people in your network if they know someone who can assist in the area you need help in. For example, if you want to be coached on presenting more effectively, seek a person who is excellent in this arena. If you want to be better at developing a high-performing team, connect with someone who can give you those pointers.

Another method, which will cost some bucks, is to hire a professional coach. Unlike mentors, there are scores of professional life coaches who specialize in all types of themes. If you go this route, it's a good idea to identify three prospective coaches, discuss what you're seeking, and then choose the one you trust, feel comfortable with, sense a strong connection with, and believe will give you the best advice. Keep in mind here that you want to hire the person who will be direct and not merely nice because you are paying them.

So now you know the difference between a mentor, a sponsor/advocate, and a coach. And now, as Steve Jobs would say, "But wait, there's more!"

What is a mole for?

MOLES LISTEN FOR YOU.

In addition to having a mentor, sponsor/advocate, and/or coach, I have come to the conclusion that everyone also needs a mole to round things out. And just what is a mole? It's a person with whom you share mutual trust who listens *for* you, and who will tell you what others say about you when you're not in the room. This may sound sneaky, but in a corporate environment, it can be crucial to have someone be your eyes and ears and to provide on-the-ground, at-the-moment intelligence you can't gain yourself.

Like the other members of your support system, a mole is not your friend. Yes, they care about your well-being and have your best interest at heart, but this person is more like a personal private investigator. They may intersect with you on projects or be in the same department or on the same floor, but in one way or another, they are intertwined in your business activities with a view of you from where they sit. Moles can be strategically positioned in places such as a promotion committee, a talent review session, or even hidden in the audience when you are presenting. It's like having your personal army of spies out there just for you.

When I worked as an executive, I had a number of moles in my professional network I used quite often to help me understand what people were saying about me. This was a highly effective way for me to get information from multiple sources, which ultimately helped me not only do the job better, but also improve on areas regarding my presentation and communication style. I would not have been aware of these opportunities if I didn't have moles.

One area that was a rude, but necessary, awakening for me was my reputation of being a jokester. As the head of diversity, it was important for me to be taken seriously, to have a commanding presentation style, and for people to believe what I said. As an influencer, I had to exhibit a high level of professionalism with internal and external stakeholders. Yet I was the one who made jokes or said something funny no matter what the situation was, regardless of who was in the room, to the point where my colleagues expected it from me. But I began hearing from my moles that people were saying I should temper my comedic style and use more discretion when I made jokes. On the surface, this was not a big deal, but on a larger scale this spelled trouble. My moles told me that because of this label, people were not taking me seriously. My comedy was not only overshadowing the strength of my diversity message, it was almost compromising my ability to lead the practice and essentially dumbing down the great work we were doing as a team.

Clearly, this was *not* the result I was seeking in being a comedic figure in my company, so I decided to regulate myself with respect to being funny. I confided in my moles about my personal development plan and informed them that I wanted to improve in this area and needed their help to keep me on track. I strove to use restraint when I was bursting to make a joke or throw out a witty remark, and I became a lot more serious (at least when I was presenting) and put my game face on. My moles were a good gauge for me to know if I was making progress as they observed the more serious me firsthand and updated me if the chatter about my comedic style was becoming subdued.

One day I was on a scheduled conference call to give a diversity update and discuss the firm's progress against our plan. On the call were senior leaders and, lucky for me, a few were my moles. One of the leaders asked me a question during my presentation—a perfect question for a funny response. But just as I was about to blurt out a witty reply, one of my moles messaged me and said, "Don't do it." He knew I was going to unleash a doozie of a response, which would have had everyone knee slapping, but in the long run would have tarnished my professional image. Those three words saved me.

To illustrate the bigger picture here: a mentor would have given me guidance on how I could change my behavior; a sponsor/advocate wouldn't have known this was something I was working on; and a coach would have told me to simply stop doing it. But my mole was there in the moment to give me the heads up I needed when I was about to shoot myself.

I have also played a mole for others. One of my mentees, who wanted to improve her presentation skills, was a nervous Nellie when she had to present and would almost go into shock when it was her turn to speak. No matter how much she prepared, she was not able to get her rhythm down. And the more nervous she became, the further from her presentation she veered. As her mole, I got to the meeting a little early and strategically positioned myself to be in her line of sight. Before the meeting, I told her I would signal her by rubbing my eyebrow if she was going too fast, and fold my hands together if she was on point and doing great. I also told her to include the word "pause" in her notes as another cue to manage her pace and rhythm. Let's just say she nailed it. Having me as her mole in the moment gave her the ability to adjust her style, boost her confidence, and hit a home run with her presentation.

I hope you now understand how each of these members of your support system is different. Remember that your character and performance will help these people identify and want to help you. Just remember you *can* become friends with people in your support system, but while they're serving as a professional connection, don't expect them to accept an invitation to your family reunion or invite you to their child's wedding. As time passes and you move on or they leave the firm—unless you keep in touch with them— they will become history (or rather, 'her'story . . . I couldn't resist!) but have an important place when you talk about your successful career and the impact they had on you.

Although I've now retired, I continue to seek out people in my personal and past professional life to be in my circle. My life has changed, but my need to have a support system has not. And because my nature is to be a giver, I still look for people who may wish to include me in their support system. It feels good to pay it forward.

In closing, I suggest you think of this support system as your board of directors. Every company has one, and if you think of yourself as the CEO of *you*, it would stand to reason you should have people in your circle you can reach out to as well. Heck, even the smartest people in the firm need some guidance as business challenges come up. So, think about who should be on your board. And remember: mentors speak *with* you, sponsor/advocates speak *for* you, coaches speak *to* you, moles listen *for* you . . . and friends let you sleep on their couch.

Ladies Only

☀

The "Old Boys' Network" is a real thing.

I was reading a research paper about coaching and mentoring when I had a "holy crap" moment. The punchline was, "Women and minorities need coaching and mentoring earlier and longer than men." I had to read that a few times: *earlier and longer*. I was mid-career when I came upon this intel, and it was like making my mom's carrot cake and finding out just before I put it in the oven that I was supposed to add vegetable oil early in the mix to meld longer in the batter. All I could do at that point was backfill to try to make up the time.

Many, if not all, of the Davidisms throughout the book and in this chapter can also be used by men. However, in my experience as a chief diversity officer, and as a technology executive working in a corporate environment—*and* being a lady myself—I have learned, lived, and observed a series of, let's just call them "things" that are either harder to do for women, don't come naturally, or are simply more acute when we don't do them as it pertains to our careers. And if we don't do these "things" relentlessly, they slow us down or keep us back, *way* back. Unfortunately, the first time we learn any of these lessons is usually when it's almost too late (aka, you call Pat!).

The bottom line is, you can't *see* this imbalance, but it's *there*.

Wikipedia defines the Old Boys' Network as referring to *"an informal system of friendships and connections through which men use their positions of influence by providing favors and information to help other men."* Okay, so Wikipedia isn't a rock solid source, but this really is a thing—and all of the new men being born are included! It's like a perpetual network that never ends. (By the way, if you search for Old Girls' Network on Wikipedia, you get: "This page does not exist.")

I have always joked with my colleagues, even to this day, that never once have I been involved with, seen, or heard of men having to create groups to meet and exchange ideas, or organizing a conference to provide men a vehicle to develop professional networks. I've also never seen talent development programs for men to provide them with an advocate or access to informal networks. Not once. Why is this? Because they don't need them! I actually came across a research report that said that men in every corner of the world, regardless of their cultural persuasion or background, are generally accepted everywhere simply because they are men. They don't even have to work on being in the informal network because it's assumed from birth. (I used to joke that maybe because as young men they peed together, so there is nothing to hide!) This has always gnawed at me when it comes to women and men in the workplace.

When I was the head of diversity, I had access to a host of information: surveys about what women believe the barriers are for advancement compared to men; research regarding the differences of communication styles between women and men; what women do to sabotage their career; the value of mentoring and coaching and why women and minorities need these earlier and longer; the list goes on and on. In the beginning I wondered, *Where was all of this information when I started out in my career? How come the guidance counselor in college didn't prepare me for these things?*

I also had access to processes in that position, such as the promotion process, the talent development process, and other people processes that gave me a birds-eye view into how people move up and out within an organization. For example: How does Pat get passed over for VP and George get it, when Pat has worked as hard and as long? How does George get identified as having potential and have the firm invest in him, and Pat continues to work hard and smart and does not get recognized? Well, I was in a position to observe how these things actually happened, and I therefore acquired knowledge. My mom used to say, "Knowledge is power." So I want to use my power to give you knowledge so *you* can have power too.

As soon as I learned about the importance of mentors and coaches, I began to abundantly share this newfound secret of success. I was like Oprah: "You get a mentor! You get a mentor!" This is why I devoted a lot of my time to high school– and college-age women—to urge them not to wait to build their network. My daughter and her friends were a perfect audience and became victim to my new information. Every time they came over, I schooled them in understanding the importance of developing relationships. And as much as my daughter would "Ma!" me to death, they appreciated it. Now today, as early-career professionals, they thank me for that guidance and even reach out from time to time for more Davidisms.

Discrimination aside, what is it that differentiates women in the workplace and beyond? Are we more suspicious of each other? Are we more judgmental of each other than men are? Possibly. I admit I've been known to display that unfavorable trait myself, as much as I hate to admit it.

I was once invited to a fancy schmancy awards luncheon during the workday at a fancy schmancy hotel. When we walked into the ballroom, many people, like us, were dressed in business suits because we had come straight from the office, but my eyes gravitated to one woman who was about six feet tall in five-inch heels. Her dress was practically painted on, she showed no visible signs of cellulite, and she looked absolutely stunning. I leaned over to my colleague and said, "Who does she think she is, Miss America or something?" It really bugged me that she looked that good, in the middle of the day, no less.

After lunch, the awards portion commenced and the emcee invited up the guest of honor. The next thing I knew, the woman I was making fun of headed up to the stage. Even in those stiletto heels, she walked flawlessly through the room and up the stairs (God forgive me, but all I could think of was, *Please trip . . . and not just a little tiny trip, but one that will give me some comfort you are human*). When she faced the audience, she had a huge sash around her body that read: Miss America. I sank into my seat so far that I nearly blended with it.

What had I done? What so many other women on this earth did all the time: I passed judgment on one of my own. I looked at her shoes, her hair, her clothes and determined she was somehow worthy of my scorn. Shame on me. Well, I vowed after that that never again would I stoop so low. In fact, I now make it my mission to never say anything bad about a woman. (I may think it, but I won't say it . . . I am human, after all.)

I tell this story because sometimes we can be our own worst enemies. If we just helped and supported each other like men do, we could build a sisterhood that crossed continents, one that would be strong enough to guide and nurture us through life. And maybe one day when you search Wikipedia for the term "sisterhood," it won't just come up as a simple definition; it will be an ongoing page of examples of how it has empowered the world.

Okay, okay . . . enough of that. But there *is* a lot of research that supports the notion that women need to begin building networks earlier and longer. It's unfortunate, but as of now, we *do* still have to work a little harder to be recognized and accepted—and those in the non-majority groups have to sometimes work twice as hard merely to be at the same pace. So as a woman (even though I was a tomboy growing up), I say, please please please absorb this chapter and then take action.

Lean against the wall.

If you look at my picture in the back of the book, you might ask, "How does a kid who looked like Buckwheat (and maybe still does) get to be the head of diversity for one of the best firms on the planet?"

When I look back and think about my journey, I would say it's part luck, part hard work, part prayer, and maybe even part stupidity (not knowing any better). I had a view that hard work would move my career along at a steady pace, and that the first firm I worked with would be the last. Well ladies, that's not exactly the way to go about managing your career.

This is how I came to recommend that you lean against the wall and what I mean by that.

For eight years after college, I worked at Philip Morris. All I did at the beginning of my career there was work hard, put in the time, and accept extra work, thinking that someone would notice and raise me up. As I mentioned earlier, when I finally picked my head up from working, I noticed there were a lot of people I started with who were moving forward because they were networking. They were literally leaning up against the wall and chatting people up. In doing this, they became known and visible, while I was unknown and invisible. So I started leaning against the wall and chatting people up. I not only made sure I was interesting, but I showed interest in who I was talking to. It didn't take long before people started to reach out to me for project work, as well as for my views on ideas they had—and all because I had begun to "lean against the wall."

Don't settle.

Years after my Philip Morris job, when I was at Salomon Brothers and was eligible to become a managing director, my boss came into my office to tell me why I wasn't getting promoted that particular year. He explained that this other person, who happened to be a man, was more eligible than I was because of tenure, and that this promotion was something he had been asking for and expecting for a while. At the time, I had a good relationship with my boss and let him get away with "giving me a heads up" and "comforting me" that next year would be my turn. I thanked him and went about my business; I figured if it was not my turn, then I should wait because the company and my boss knew best.

In other words, I settled.

Yes, I *did* get the promotion the following year. But I also not only reminded my boss of his promise (thankfully, he remained my boss that year), I reminded him of my expectation—and my excellent work backed me up.

That experience taught me to ask for everything and anything I believe I deserve in life and business. Let it do the same for you.

:☼:

You will be sought after if your work stands out.

I was once asked by my boss's secretary to come to his staff meeting. I was thinking, *What now?* I walked into the meeting and all of his direct reports were there, and each of them promptly stared at me. I wondered if I had toilet paper on my shoe or if something that shouldn't be showing was showing! Then my boss proceeded to tell me that the senior managers had been talking and decided to launch an employee involvement committee. This would be a forum where employees could share ideas on how to improve their experience, as well as a place to get employees engaged around firm-wide efforts and the like, and they needed a person to champion this effort and take the lead. All I could think was, *What does this have to do with me? All I want to do is come to the office, work, and go home.* Turned out they summoned me because they wanted *me* to lead this committee, which only existed in name.

"Why me?" I asked.

"Because your work stands out, you're well respected by employees, and you don't bring any drama" was the answer.

Now, you have to understand that as a brown-skinned female in corporate America, I was a unicorn at times, and because of that I was always being either judged or inspected. But the one thing that was undeniable was my work. I don't care what the industry is or how big or small the company is, they all want one thing: to cultivate the best team to do the work they will be measured on. Managers are therefore often looking for people to do the work in order for them to get the credit, and they are always hunting for talent. And yes, managers (at least the good ones) are also looking to help others move up and achieve their potential.

Every one of the people who helped me progress in my career sought me out because my work spoke for itself. In this particular case, this was the beginning of my experience in employee engagement, diversity, volunteering, and a host of other activities that I grew to excel in, which prepared me for the senior diversity roles I held that made up the best years of my professional career.

So remember: you never know when someone is watching you or looking for talent, so always, and I mean always, do good work and never leave a firestorm in your wake.

Trust others to guide you.

When I worked for Citigroup, I met with my boss for my annual performance review at the end of the year, and during that conversation he asked me a question I was not prepared for. "What else do you want to do at the firm?" This was not a question I was used to getting, and certainly not one I was used to answering. I thought about it for a nanosecond then blurted out, "I would like a position as head of diversity." I said this because the woman in the role at the time always looked happy. I added that I would also like to be the head of communications because the firm had been good to me, and it would be great to use that platform to help others feel the same way about the company. I also said that any role where I could inter-act with employees directly 85 to 90 percent of the time would be great. Working in technology, there was always something that needed to be fixed, re-viewed, or renewed, so there was a lot of interaction with software, vendors, and lines of code but very little interaction with people. Mind you, none of the ideas I blurted out were in my boss's line of responsibil-ity, so I was essentially saying I would like a role working with people—and oh, by the way, I'll have to leave you if this actually happens because positions like that report to HR. Luckily, I had a great relation-ship with my boss, so this was not awkward to propose.

After my performance conversation, we both signed the review and it was filed away, never to be seen again—or so I thought. The next thing I knew, I got a call from the head of HR saying he heard I was interested in the head of diversity role. So now I'm thinking, *How did my secret conversation with my boss get out there? Did someone read my review?*

What happened was that three months after my performance review, the head of diversity resigned. During a meeting where senior leaders and HR were reviewing candidates for the position, my boss put my name on the slate. Since the head of human re-sources only knew one side of me, he questioned it, saying, "Isn't she a techie?" But shortly after, I began getting calls from my network of ladies and senior leaders encouraging me to consider the role. To be honest, I wasn't sure what being the head of diversity entailed, nor did I think I had the expertise or stomach for it. And when I asked my supporters about the expectations and skills needed for the role, let's just say I heard radio silence. You see, at that time and even now, this is not a job you find in every company. And even if you do, they are so varied that it's impossible to pin down what's involved. I was not only filled with doubt and uncertainty about taking a visible role without much, if any, idea as to what the job encompassed, I was also ensconced in my comfort zone and not even looking for another position. And I was *triple* not going to take the job if the firm wanted me to play the role of black female activist. Nope, not my cup of tea. In fact, I turned the job down three times before I finally accepted the position.

When I thought about it, there was so much support for me to take on this role that I almost could not fail. Yes, I had been reluctant, but what I realized is that these people could see something in me I couldn't see in myself. If I hadn't listened to them, I would have passed up one of the best jobs I ever had.

The Davidism here is that you need to have trust when a senior person recommends that you consider an opportunity and believes you can do it. In this situation, take their advice. You may well find that you learn to trust those who believe in you, maybe more than you believe in yourself.

If not me, then who?

I have a new mantra for you that goes like this: "Someone will [get a raise, get promoted, get more exposure]. If not me, then who?" Saying this allows you a shift in attitude to where you can focus on believing in yourself. You *can* achieve and succeed, but it has to start with you.

Take a deep breath, then exhale out all the noise and drama and naysayers and disbelievers who may be in your life who pull you back instead of raise you up. If you believe you have just as much opportunity and choice as anyone else, put your back into it and take what is yours.

Labels, Labels, Labels

Quite often, women will share with me that her boss doesn't think she is strategic enough, technical enough, whatever enough—and that's why she didn't get a promotion. When she asks them to explain and give details on what that means so she can improve, the response is vague. So she makes great efforts—takes courses, reads books, teaches herself to fill the gap— to show the boss she is the thing he/she thinks she's not. These things may be fine to do, but my advice is always: *Change how you describe yourself.*

Here's what I mean.

On your resume, use descriptors you want to be known for. In meetings, when you ask a question, start out by saying, "I was thinking strategically . . ." or "From a technical perspective . . ." You'd be surprised how your labels change to the ones you want once you start to use them often. This is all part of managing your brand.

I once coached a woman who wanted to make sure the client and her peers treated her with respect for the extensive knowledge and experience she had prior to joining this particular group, where she used to manage a team and had a fair amount of power and authority. This new position she was in gave her access to quite a number of people, but for the first few years, she was given work that was below her skill set. Because she wanted to be known as a person who managed large teams and could think strategically, I told her to adopt the habit that whenever she spoke and wanted to make a point, to begin with the words, "I was strategically thinking . . ." or "When I was a boss and managed XX of people supporting YY clients . . ." After a short time of doing this, her client started calling her "the boss."

This tactic is a no-cost way to create the right labels you want attributed to you. You just have to work at defining the labels you want to describe yourself, and then start using them, everywhere.

If you want to know what labels best suit you, ask

some close business colleagues, family members, or friends. Because they see you in your natural state, they will provide you with information that is invaluable. When I tried this with my daughter, asking how she would describe me in one word, she responded (pretty quickly I might add): *talker*. This was a label I liked (I actually saw being a talker as my superpower), so I was not about to work on changing it. When I asked my boss, he described me as an executer—a person who gets things done (not someone who bumps people off). This was another label I liked. Then a friend gave me another label: comedian. This was a great one to have at home or around family and friends, but as I've already mentioned, as the head of diversity it was not so appropriate. Can you imagine your head of diversity being considered a comedian? How serious do you think people would take her? I can hear the schtick now as she tries to warm up the room before presenting an update: "Hey, did you hear the one about the Black guy, the Hispanic, and the veteran who meet Jesus in a bar?" So, to be certain I was perceived appropriately in my role, I worked on that label so I could still be myself but dial it back when I needed to. Yes, I still made jokes, but I wasn't the headliner at meetings anymore. And when I was delivering something serious, I sometimes started a sentence by saying, "I have an important point I'm going to make, so I need your undivided attention."

This Davidism is a reminder that if you don't like

the labels attached to you, you are obligated to work on rebranding yourself.

Don't tire yourself out, delegate!

Ever wonder why women always seem to be busy and rarely relaxing? It's because our brains are wired to get things done, and when we're finished getting things done, we find other things to do. We repeat this mad cycle over and over and over again.

After years of observing this pattern, I had an aha moment: If you ask a woman to do something, the first thing she does is think about how she's going to do it—she writes a list, makes a timeline, schedules a meeting, etc. If you ask a man to do something, the first thing he does is try to figure out whom he can find to get it done.

The truth is, most of the time, the requestor couldn't care less who does the task; they're just concerned about it getting done. So the message here is: Don't tire yourself out by assuming you have to do everything. Delegating certain tasks not only frees you up to do more important things, it also gives others a chance to show their value and to shine.

:☀:
Learn from your mistakes.

Women, in particular, have a problem moving past mistakes. Worse, they tend to refer to them, and worse yet, continuously remind people of them. If this describes you, it is a habit you *must* break immediately. Not only does it degrade you unnecessarily with yourself and others, it limits your growth. Think about it: if you are too risk averse, you won't be challenged enough to have the opportunity to learn. Something will always break or go wrong, and you'll have to walk into your boss's office and explain the problem. But what should follow that explanation is confidence that you can handle it, and what ideas you have to solve it. And once you have solved it, move on.

:☀:
Protect what is yours.

Have you had your work or your words ripped off, either sent around as if someone else had done it or been quoted in a meeting? Instead of storming around or silently fuming, here's how you can deal with it like a calm and cool pro.

A colleague steals your idea or report and sends it out to people and cc's you:
Send a response to everyone saying something to

the effect of: "Thank you [shark's name] for sending the report I prepared for the group. If anyone has any questions about the information, please feel free to call me."

You're in a meeting and someone says what you've already stated but louder:

Follow up with: "[shark's name], I'm glad you also agree with my point and would further add xx." Or, "Thanks, [shark's name], for framing my position more succinctly. It's great to have your support on this issue." Or, "It's great to know you support and agree with my thought process."

See how much more effective this is than watching your idea get stolen and then complaining after everyone leaves the room?

An added funny story on this topic . . .

One day, my younger sister was going to cut my older sister's hair in the bathroom. My mom and I were in the kitchen when my older sister came crying to my mom, "Look what Cookie did to my hair." My mom coolly responded, "Weren't you there?"

The lesson: Instead of getting upset about something after the fact, protect what is yours in the moment.

By the way, her hair looked terrible.

☀

Godspeed.

At times it may feel like you're carrying a heavy bag—even if it's a Michael Kors, a Louis Vuitton, a Coach, or even a Birkin. But, ladies, you have arrived. Take your place in the business world. This is our time! The possibilities for what you can achieve are endless—don't let anyone make you feel otherwise.

With that in mind, here are a few things to hold fast to as you conquer the world.

* Be disciplined in running your business and taking care of your brand.

* Set high standards—and if you achieve them, raise them even higher.

* Race against yourself, not your competitor.

* See the big picture and move toward it every day.

* Have conviction for what you believe in.

You are part of a generation of women who have the responsibility to make things better on your watch, so grab the reins. The world needs you to transform it—this is why I call this section "Godspeed," which is the equivalent of saying, "Go forward already!"

You know that old saying: "Work like a dog,

think like a man, and act like a lady"? Well, the "think like a man" part gnaws at me. It's been decades that women have stood up to vote, gotten educated, and led countries and companies, so why should we have to think like a man? I call BS on that. Full stop.

Almost on a daily basis at work, I was asked if we as women were making progress. What people really wanted to know was: Are the numbers improving? Are women represented equally or better than men as we move up in the organization? Are women equally represented at the CEO level running fortune 500 companies? Are more women heads of nations?

These are all good questions, but if the numbers aren't moving fast enough, I recommend reading the following article, written for male supervisors of women in the workforce during World War II, called "1943 Guide to Hiring Women." (I like to grab a glass of red wine and something chocolatey, or a huge bucket of buttered popcorn, and put my feet up while I read it.) By the time I'm done, I have a smile on my face from ear to ear! Now it's your turn to read it and to decide if we are making progress.

Eleven Tips on Getting More Efficiency Out of Women Employees

There's no longer any question whether transit companies should hire women for jobs formerly held by men. The draft and manpower shortage has settled that point. The important things now are to select the most efficient women available and how to use them to the best advantage. Here are eleven helpful tips on the subject from western properties:

1. If you can get them, pick young married women. They have these advantages, according to the reports of western companies: they usually have more of a sense of responsibility than do their unmarried sisters, they're less likely to be flirtatious, they need the work or they wouldn't be doing it, they still have the pep and interest to work hard and to deal with the public efficiently.

2. When you have to use older women, try to get ones who have worked outside the home at some time in their lives. Most transportation companies have found that older women who have never contacted the public have a hard time adapting themselves and are inclined to be cantankerous and fussy. It's always well to impress upon older women the importance of friendliness and courtesy.

3. General experience indicates that "husky" girls — those who are just a little on the heavy side — are likely to be more even tempered and efficient than their underweight sisters.

4. Retain a physician to give each woman you hire a special physical examination — one covering female conditions. This step not only protects the property against the possibilities of lawsuit, but reveals whether the employee-to-be has any female weaknesses which would make her mentally or physically unfit for the job.

5. Stress at the outset the importance of time and the fact that a minute or two lost here and there makes serious inroads on schedules. Until this point is gotten across, service is likely to be slowed up.

6. Give the female employee a definite day-long schedule of duties so that she'll keep busy without bothering the management for instructions every few minutes. Numerous properties say that women make excellent workers when they have their jobs cut out for them, but that they lack initiative in finding work themselves.

7. Whenever possible, let the inside employee change from one job to another at some time during the day. Women are inclined to be less nervous and happier with change.

8. Give every girl an adequate number of rest periods during the day. You have to make some allowances for feminine psychology. A girl has more confidence and is more efficient if she can keep her hair tidied, apply fresh lipstick and wash her hands several times a day.

9. Be tactful in issuing instructions or in making criticisms. Women are often sensitive; they can't shrug off harsh words the way men do. Never ridicule a woman — it breaks her spirit and cuts off her efficiency.

10. Be reasonably considerate about using strong language around women. Even though a girl's husband or father may swear vociferously, she'll grow to dislike a place of business where she hears too much of this.

11. Get enough size variety in operator's uniforms that each girl can have a proper fit. This point can't be stressed too much in keeping women happy.

You can't make this stuff up!

My advice, ladies? Make long-term decisions about your career by defining it, describing it, then doing it.

Summer Interns Only

If this chapter fits where you are on your journey, please grab a pen and notepad and take some notes. If not, feel free to skip to the next chapter—or to enjoy the perspective from a leadership point of view.

If you are fortunate enough to be accepted into a ten-week summer internship, there are a number of things you need to do to get yourself ready, as well as to maximize your chances of receiving the coveted offer for either another summer or a full-time position in a program.

Let's start by looking at some numbers you've probably never thought about.

A standard job interview lasts about thirty to forty minutes. But a summer internship lasts anywhere from nine to ten weeks, which means your "interview"—or showing a company how well you can perform—will last from 21,600 to 24,000 minutes. In other words, this summer gig is the longest interview you'll have in your entire life. So, if you hope to receive an offer after the internship ends, you'll need to approach it with a lot more structure and focus than you would for a thirty-minute interview.

Let's level set before we get into the Davidisms.

Here is the scenario. You receive a call from a recruiter and are told you have an interview with company X on Monday, January 3rd, at 3:00 p.m. at their corporate office, located at 100 Main Street, USA. You will be meeting with Jane Doe, the hiring manager. What do you do?

You probably smile from ear to ear, happy you got the interview, then plan your attack. You review the job description and perhaps jot down why you would be a great hire. You do an online search about the company; you also research Jane Doe and see if someone in your network knows her so you can get more information about her management style. You might even ask someone in your network to put in a good word for you. You then spend about three or four hours preparing and practicing what you're going to say, what you're going to wear, and some questions you are planning on asking. Then, the day before the interview, you review your notes. The day of the interview you arrive 15–30 minutes early, ready, motivated, and engaged for what's going to happen within the next hour. You are on your best behavior and make sure that for the thirty minutes you're with

Jane, she sees you as the perfect candidate for her position. By the time you leave the interview, you have a pretty good sense of how you did and what the next steps are in terms of meeting a few more people. You handwrite her a thank-you note and mail it right after the interview. Easy as pie, right?

Now let's change the scenario.

You get a call from a recruiter and are told you have been accepted into Company X's summer intern program. It's a nine-week position that begins on June 21st, at 9:00 a.m., at the corporate office. Your goal is to do a great job and secure a full-time offer after the internship is over. The question now is, can you repeat how you presented yourself to Jane Doe for thirty minutes, approximately sixteen times a day, for nine weeks? I know that sounds like a hefty assignment, but that is exactly what you have to do.

To help you get your mind around that, here is an easy way to strategize and increase your chances of getting that coveted offer. As preparation similar to the thirty-minute interview example, do some research on the company and, if possible, on the person or team you will be working with.

Maximizing Your Internship

You'll want to break down your nine weeks into thirds, building on your experience with each successive three weeks.

FIRST THREE WEEKS

Look down. This means coming in fully engaged, being attentive to the details of what you are being asked to do and the timing of what is due when, and executing on those expectations. You want to focus on coming into work every day and showing your manager they hired the right intern for the summer. Here are four things to keep in mind to demonstrate that.

* Work as if every email you send, every task you do, every meeting you attend, and every time you open your mouth, you are being watched and evaluated. Because guess what? You are. Everything you do, say, and write is part of the nine-week interview.

* Show the firm you have what it takes to work in the industry.

* Seek out others each week to get to know people in the group.

* Ask questions—it shows you are listening. Ask for clarity on a task you are working on, on what certain acronyms stand for, on anything relevant to your assignments. Make it a point to say something every single day— it's the only way your boss knows you have a brain. And if you don't have a question on a particular topic, make a comment that shows you've been paying attention.

* Display your maturity and professionalism.
  The way you dress and the way you carry
  yourself will go a long way. Imagine dressing
  for your first interview every day—in
  whatever the "uniform" is for the firm—from
  your clothes to your hair to your shoes to
  your nails. In other words, dress like you are
  already a member of the team.

SECOND THREE WEEKS

Look up. As you learn more about how things operate,
you'll want to connect with others and begin to understand how your work is connected to the group.

* While continuing to exhibit the habits and
  behaviors already stated, expand your actions
  by asking questions regarding what other
  groups do and where the tasks you are
  working on fit into the firm. Speak from a
  position of curiosity and being inquisitive.

* Expand your knowledge by doing some more
  research on the industry and the firm—
  explore the company website further, if you
  haven't already, follow the company through
  various credible media outlets, and start to
  act more like an employee.

* Again, continue to ask questions. You need to
  be asking a question or regurgitating

something you heard or learned every day so that your manager hears what you are thinking.

* Continue to seek out others each week to get to know people in the group.

LAST THREE WEEKS

Look outward. This means networking and developing relationships. After you've had some time in the firm, you'll want to identify people you want to stay in touch with professionally (not everyone you've worked with will qualify).

* Start to think about the people you have met and establish a list of key individuals. This does not mean collecting business cards or going to every event and being the last to leave. It means keeping an eye out for people you have met you want to continue to speak with and get to know.

* On or before your last day, make an effort to meet with your manager and other key people in your area. Shake their hands and thank them for the opportunity to work with them (this will make you memorable). Give them a few tidbits of what this opportunity has taught you, and let them know you are more than interested in starting your career

at that firm (provided you indeed have interest in working for them).

* Reach out to the HR person who onboarded you and echo your interest to start your career at the firm. Thank them for the opportunity.

* Find out what the next steps are for keeping in touch or knowing about job opportunities.

* Keep in touch (not every day, but every few months) with your new network. You can send an article you read that you want to share, or something you worked on in school that was similar to the work you did over the summer. Either way, make the connection meaningful instead of just saying "Hey" in an email. (By the way, never start an email, under any condition, with "Hey.")

By breaking your time into these three segments, you can better strategize how to maximize your nine weeks—which will go by in a flash. And there are no do-overs, so embrace the goal of having a quick start and a strong finish by Looking Down, Looking Up, and Looking Outward!

Additional Tips for an Optimum Experience

AS WITH YOUR SHORT INTERVIEW:

* Come to work a few minutes early each day.

* Don't leave until you are dismissed.

* Send a thank-you note expressing your interest, as well as thanking the person you reported to for their time in training and working with you.

IN CONTRAST TO THE SHORT INTERVIEW:

* Don't expect everyone you meet to be nice to you. **During the short interview,** you were on the outside looking in, and there were likely a lot of pleasantries. **During your internship,** you are being integrated into the department and people are going to rely on you, treat you like a member of the team, and expect you to add value.

* **During the short interview,** you have only a few hours to assess the culture of the company and size up the people you meet. **During your internship,** you have hundreds of hours to determine if the culture is really right for you—and the company has a lot more time to size you up too!

THINGS TO KEEP IN MIND DURING YOUR INTERNSHIP YOU MIGHT NOT HAVE CONSIDERED:

* The firm and/or the industry may experience some challenges during your time there—organizational changes, missteps, and the like. In other words, a lot can change while you are there; the key is to see how the firm and your team handle these issues. Did it pose a problem for you? Did you feel comfortable with the staff interactions under pressure?

* Don't assume you have to go to every outside networking event—you will not be measured on how many you attend, but you *will* be expected to carry yourself as a professional when you *do* attend. This goes for the requisite number of luncheons, town halls, team meetings, and for social or volunteering activities as well.

* Don't confuse a "meet and greet" with a "stay and talk." These conversations and times with senior people are precious, so be prepared when you are meeting someone and try to keep the time to thirty minutes or less. DO plan to have a conversation where you sound interested in what is said and being interesting when you speak. DON'T walk into a person's office all cheery, plop yourself

in a chair, and expect the person you are meeting to carry the conversation.

* You're in a professional environment, so don't be too casual with relationships and conversations. And while you're at it, make sure every email is professional and not too informal. Remember, emails are the firm's property, so assume every email you write is being read by someone other than the person you intended to send it to.

* Don't feel the need to smile and say hello every time you see a person throughout the day. It's actually annoying and childish.

* Your physical presentation should not be a distraction. Remember, you are being interviewed every single day, so make sure you look the part. As I mentioned in an earlier chapter, you should not be heard or smelt before you are seen, meaning your clothes should not jingle, your shoes should not make flip-flop noises, and you should not reek of body spray. Some of you may find this advice a little jarring, but I have seen people come to work in the summer with strappy sandals or stilettos, and neither are good after being on your feet for eight to ten hours. I have also witnessed young women wearing lovely hoop earrings that were as big as actual

Hula Hoops, or young men coiffed to the nines with so much Paco Rabanne cologne that you'd think he was just sprayed by the perfume lady at a department store! The point is, it's always best to go conservative, unless the company and its people present themselves otherwise.

* And last, *do not* spend your internship merely collecting a paycheck (if it's paid) or showing up for eight hours to simply fulfill the required time (if it's not paid). If you do that, don't expect to get an offer. That level of disengagement will almost certainly inhibit your ability to return to the firm the next summer (or receive an offer) because the firm will remember you as a rock, not a rock star!

The Big 7 Derailers

During my years interacting with the summer interns who made it and who didn't, I discovered some clear derailers that can be avoided and increase your chances of getting an offer. I call them "The Big 7," and I'm listing them here so that you can stay clear of them.

1. **BEING DISENGAGED.** You must act like you want to be there, both physically and through your actions and words.

2. **OVER-NETWORKING.** As I said, you will not be reviewed and measured on the number of events you went to and business cards you collected. The work comes first—don't forget it.

3. **NOT ASKING QUESTIONS.** As I've already said, it's imperative that you ask a question every single day—and if you don't have one, either find openings to make a comment or to ask someone to confirm you understand what you're doing or what was said in a meeting. You must speak!

4. **STARTING LATE.** Although the internship is about nine weeks long, you must bring your A-game on day one. If you wait until after the first week, it's too late. It's game time every single day.

5. **DEBATING YOUR PERFORMANCE.** Performance discussions are a professional, mature exchange between you and your manager, so when you have your mid-summer review and receive development feedback, don't disagree or cop an attitude with what you're being told. Accept the feedback, say thank you, and show evidence within 24 hours that you heard the feedback and are acting on whatever you were told to improve upon.

6. **NOT BEING RESPONSIBLE.** You may see yourself as "just" an intern (though an earlier Davidism reminded you never to be "just" anything!), but the

work you do matters and the team is expecting you to play your position. So, remember to act like a responsible adult. Whatever they ask you to do needs to get done, so do it!

7. **NOT OWNING MISTAKES.** When you make a mistake, don't try to hide it or hope with time it will go away. The key is to quickly show that you own up to it and then work on ways to not allow it to happen again. Everyone makes mistakes. The test is how you handle them.

Manage Your Brand on Social Media

You probably don't need me to tell you that good, bad, or indifferent, your social media presence amplifies your brand. In my generation, someone had to find a yearbook, a document, or some physical evidence they could piece together to get a character reference. Today, finding information about you is as easy as going online and doing a search.

Think about it: if someone wanted to create a character reference of you, and all they did was review your Linked-In profile, Facebook and Instagram posts, and TikTok videos, what would the report say about you? Or what if someone wanted to create a profile of you and what you value, and they only looked at the things you "like," the "friends" you are connected to online, and the tweets you've made, what kind of person would they determine you are?

I recently heard about a young lady not getting admitted into a prestigious college because a "friend" of hers posted a video of her using the "n" word. In another instance, a person was asked to step down from a management position because they went to a costume party in blackface. In both cases, I don't think either person expected that moment in their past would make a difference in their future, but it damn well did. So please be mindful of what you put out there on social media because it's accessible to everyone—and bosses don't hesitate to keep up on the caliber of their employees by checking on them periodically through their social media platforms.

And one more thing: if you have any sketchy "friends" who tag you in a photo, that could have negative repercussions for you too. Make sure your "friends" get your permission to tag you in photos. The last thing you need/want is to be in a photo with the appearance of doing something inappropriate. And deleting something does not permanently delete it—it just makes it harder for people to find. Plus, by the time you delete something, someone may have already forwarded it with a catchy GIF to make the scenario even worse, and you probably don't even know it happened. So take extra care of your brand, starting now.

Take It Off the Table

The last subject I want to address for you interns is what happens when you receive an offer. It could be a no-brainer Yes! But what if you were exceptional during your summer internship and you didn't get only one, but *two* full-time job offers? Which offer do you accept? Before this happens, it's a good idea to identify the criteria you will use to decide so that you don't spend a lot of time and call a ton of people to help you overanalyze each offer before you make a decision.

You should know by now that most full-time offers for interns are generally the same, at least when it comes to salary and title, so obviously these cannot be deciding factors. However, there will be some things about each offer that will be different, and you'll need to weigh these differences to help you decide which offer to take, or none at all.

Some of the criteria could be:

* location of the role
* team dynamics
* travel expectations
* work hours
* benefits
* overall company fit

What I want you to do is make your own list. Now, "take off the table" the things that, for you, would not make a difference either way. What's left is only the criteria that's most important to you, and that's what you'll use to decide between the offers (provided there *is* some difference between the two within your remaining criteria). If you've already done your homework, it should be pretty easy to choose. (By the way, this is the same advice I give to seasoned professionals as they change jobs or careers.)

Here's an example of what this might look like.

Of your two offers, one of the positions is similar to one you did before and would not help to move your career forward, while the other is in an exciting field and pays a bit less but is in an industry you want to explore. After weighing your pros and cons about both positions, nothing tips one over the other except one major factor: you are anti anything that looks or smells like something you did before, to the point where you actually sound whiny when you talk about it. (Here's where I ask, "Why did you interview for a position you knew you wouldn't want?") But I digress . . .

Knowing this one isn't going to align with your goals or interests, it's easy to then take this offer off the table. Why hang on to empty options that can stress you out and almost cripple your judgment? This is why you need to only include the variables that matter and the choices you would actually consider, then make a decision and move forward. Don't be the woulda, coulda, shoulda person.

Here is another example.

When my kids were applying to college, I told them to only apply to schools they would actually choose if they were accepted, and then to prioritize their favorite. So, if they applied to five colleges, they were agreeing to attend any of the five. I never understand why a kid applies to twenty colleges. If it's just to prove a point, it's a pretty expensive way to show off. Doing some local community volunteer work is a much better way to show off your skills than wasting the time of multiple schools you'd never want to attend if you were accepted to them. (Sorry about the rant, but this one gets me going!)

The point is, the same strategy applies to your career and life choices. Eliminate the options you would never consider under any condition, and then make a choice from the list that remains. It's a more mature and balanced way to look at things (and can sometimes save you money, such as in college application costs!). Best of all, it reduces your choices to a manageable few where you can make an educated and informed decision, which will serve you well throughout your career.

Leaders Only

I have news for you: If you're a leader, and you turn around and no one is following you, you are merely going for a stroll! When you are truly a leader, it's your responsibility to get people fired up about potential change. (It's also your responsibility to fire people if they're not performing to the standards of the job.) When you get people excited about their jobs, you'll find that when you turn around, you won't be alone.

The scariest time in my career was when I became responsible for other people (no, not when I became a mother, but when I became a manager). My boss was leaving to join another firm and he promoted me into his position as the VP of technology at Merrill Lynch. One day I was on the team; the next day I was leading the team and responsible for it. To be honest, I kept doing the same work without changing any of my habits. The only real change I made was to have staff meetings to make sure I was aware of the status of all the projects we were responsible for and that we could deliver on time. Yes, I worked longer hours, but I never took a step back to think about how I should or could change my habits or behaviors. My team, however, *did* change—in terms of how they viewed me. The people who had just been my peers expected me to lead them, listen to them, provide them with the tools they needed, and on and on. The problem was, they thought that because I was the VP in charge, I had received full training—in the few minutes between having my old job and being given my new one—on what to do and how to do it. Not! It took a while for me to get my groove on and develop a better cadre of rituals before I hit my stride. It was not smooth and seamless, to say the least.

After that promotion, I learned a lot through the years that I would like to share with all you leaders, or future leaders, so your transitions can hopefully be smoother than mine were.

And if you're an employee and read this section, and you feel that your manager can use some of these Davidisms, please buy them a copy of the book, dog-ear these pages, and leave it on their desk. Say it's from me!

Mind the clock.

When I was younger, I rarely paid attention to time. Although I watched the clock to make sure I didn't miss my bus or a flight, I never really thought much about time in the sense of life and how little time we have on this Earth in the big scheme of things. It wasn't until my husband had a heart attack that I started to think about time differently. Only a few years after his triple bypass surgery, my younger sister passed away, followed two years later by the death of my brother, aunt, and father within months of each other. What I learned real quick is that time is the most precious of things and you can't get it back.

If I could wish for one thing it would be a time machine. But because I cannot go back in time, I am acutely focused on making sure I don't take time for granted. I've learned to not only be more efficient with my time, but not to waste other people's either.

What I began to do at work was to block out time on my calendar to think, to prepare, and to listen. I also made sure I didn't waste time on the job doing things that I could do at home or during my commute (like sleep). Just kidding! But seriously, as a leader, you need to be mindful of your time and that of others. Here are some ways I was able to maximize my time during a workday.

* I moved away from having meetings in my office so that I could leave when I wanted to.

* I started to use technology tools at my disposal to make myself more efficient, like putting tasks and reminders on my phone calendar and flagging things to follow up on.

* Meetings I conducted were always less than

an hour, and I always sent out an agenda in advance.

* I sat opposite a clock when I was in a meeting so I didn't have to keep looking at my watch.

* I had my secretary get me one of those sand clocks to keep me on schedule—when the sand ran out, it was time to go.

* I encouraged people to be on time and to be prepared. If they were late, the end time for our meeting wouldn't change. I was pretty strict with this one. Eventually, people learned to be on time—David time.

Identify your takeout.

No, I'm not talking about Door Dash or Uber Eats. I'm talking about identifying your takeout in terms of developing your successor. This is a critical action all leaders should take but very few do, perhaps because it's difficult, or because we want to do the job forever, or because we don't get measured on it in a performance review. But I want to tell you here that within three to six months of starting a new job, you need to begin looking for your replacement. By that time, you should have attended enough meetings and met enough people where you can identify a few you think would be good candidates. The key is to keep look-ing, and eventually you will have a pool of people to consider. And when you have that all-important tal-ent review discussion and your boss asks you who can replace you, or who could be your successor now or in 18 to 24 months, you won't be caught in a blank stare.

:☀:

Take compensation seriously.

A hair-raising moment for me was just a few months into my tenure as the VP of technology at Merrill Lynch. A person from HR sent me a spreadsheet with my team's compensation history, their performance ratings, and the company's compensation guidelines, and asked me to fill in what their bonus should be. *Wait, what?* I thought. *You want me to put numbers in a cell on a spreadsheet, and once I do you'll convert that to money, and each person will get that amount as their bonus?* Now, this was a serious ask, and it was the first time I realized the power I had as a manager/leader.

I always heard people say that paying people was one of the most important things a manager has to do, and here I was in the driver's seat, with only a few days to make the calculations. I kept thinking that whatever number I wrote down would be the starting point for years to come for each person, which could mean the difference between community college or

Ivy League for someone, or what food they put on the table, or the size of the mortgage they could get. I did not want to screw this up because once I sent the spreadsheet, it couldn't be undone.

As an employee, prior to my role as a manager, I'd heard enough stories from people who didn't think they got paid commensurate with their performance or that of the firm. I also heard people say they didn't get paid enough because the manager didn't like them or didn't value what they were working on. There were so many variables and things to consider to get it right, and I did *not* want to be the manager who screwed it up.

I did the best I could to look at each person's contribution, not only what they did but *how* they did it. I also looked at their work history and anything during the year that might have impacted their performance, such as personal issues, reorganizations, new projects, etc. In addition, I looked at market and peer data to determine where they would be on the continuum of their peers in similar roles with similar experiences. I did all of this so that I would have an airtight position if the employee wasn't happy; it was crucial to me to be able to explain how I came to the number because that's what I would be asked.

So, if you find yourself in the position of determining the compensation of an individual, take it seriously—because they will.

:☼:
Celebrate little successes.

Public acknowledgement is a reward that doesn't cost you any money but is invaluable to the recipient. There is nothing better than having your boss shout out your name in a crowd and share something of value you did, or to be at a town hall or staff meeting and be recognized as a team or individual who went beyond the call of duty to improve something or help someone. Sometimes what may seem like a little success to you is a big success for your team.

So, be great at celebrating even the little successes, because they truly do matter—psychological rewards and recognition go a long way in any organization.

:☼:
Care.

People will do a great job if you show you care about the job they do. It's easy to reach out to people working on a key project or who are fixing a major problem when something goes wrong and show them you have interest in what they're immersed in. Ditto for the person or team that comes in every day and supports the company in keeping the place running.

Everyone is important to the health of the organization, so make it a habit to do a little outreach or offer a compliment of thanks. Those efforts truly do go a long way.

Delegate and let them work.

I know, sometimes it's hard to let go of the work, especially if you just got promoted and are now responsible for the team you worked with for a long time. But if you keep doing the everyday tasks, you can't lead and develop the team. Worse, they won't grow, and neither will you. As hard as it is, it's vital to give your team more responsibility so they can develop, which will allow you to manage upward and outward.

I was notorious for letting my team do the work and for making sure I gave them the opportunities I'd had to showcase their skills and expand their own networks—all while giving them the credit for their accomplishments. This kept me out of their way and gave them a platform to succeed in their own right.

I need to emphasize that this is *not* about dumping all the work on your team while you sit on your throne; it's about giving out as much work as you can for *their* learning and growth—and then being fair and generous in acknowledging their contributions.

⛺

Don't make it about you. Make it about the team.

Whenever I think about the most important thing I needed to do as a manager, it boiled down to one thing: the team. It's like being a parent and providing your children with opportunities to grow and develop; indirectly, you will be fulfilled as a parent. If you operate this way, things just seem to fall into place. Focusing on *your* development, *your* promotion, *your* exposure is all well and good, but if you're not doing any of this for the team, you will fall short of achieving your goals. Why? Because the team is what got you here and will get you there, *if* you put them first.

⛺

Build high-performing teams.

As the VP of technology for financial systems at Merrill Lynch, my team was comprised of developers, network engineers, and application testers. Now mind you, I don't have a technology degree and I have never even taken a computer science course. But, I excelled at developing high-performing teams and recruiting the right people.

For one, I learned to hire people smarter than I was; in fact, I recall telling my direct reports many times to never listen to me when it came to technology ideas and solutions (that's what their responsibility was), but to tell me what tools they needed to be able to do the job. So, as their leader, I spent the majority of time getting them what they asked for to build the best systems and to develop their skills. Not having to do the work myself gave me more time to connect with senior leaders and to be included in the informal network, which allowed me to establish a strong platform to succeed as well as establish outside connections. If I had been mired in the work itself, I would not have been able to network and get the exposure I needed as a leader to get noticed. At the same time, I was ensuring the deliverables for the company by fully supporting my team's needs.

Building high-performing teams also indirectly creates an aura around them, such that your leadership style becomes almost a magnet for talent. People will want to work with the best so *they* can be the best.

Eliminate advancement constipation.

This is probably one of my most notable Davidisms. I coined this term in 2002 when I worked at Citigroup, while I was part of a high-potential talent development exercise. A senior leader and I were given the challenge to review historical employee data of a particular division, which included turnover, retention, promotion, and recruitment statistics. We had to then do an analysis and report back on how well we thought this department was doing with respect to its people.

After reviewing scores of data, we concluded that people in that particular division were doomed and stuck in their careers. Many of the employees were mid-career and had been with the firm for over five years with good reviews; recruitment at the lower levels was high compared to senior levels. But promotability and mobility were extremely low, lower than the firm-wide average.

How come no one was moving up? we wondered. It was almost as if the department was frozen in time.

The senior manager of the group touted this as a good thing, proud to share that he had long service employees and that people rarely left the group. What he failed to realize was that the reason they didn't leave was because they couldn't find their way out— there was no development plan for people to learn new skills and get experience outside of their job, and there was little to no exposure. I described this as *advancement constipation*—a problem no amount of Pepto Bismol or Drano can fix.

The Davidism here is that if you are a manager and have a similar situation, figure out a way to create mobility—and remember "up" is not the only way. And if you are the blockage causing the constipation, move! As a leader, it's your responsibility to develop your people, whether by pulling them up or pushing them out, not getting in their way. Think about the people coming up behind you and don't be a blocker. If you don't move on, you have just sealed their fate and essentially stalled their mobility.

In my experience, when this scenario plays out in business, it's always the top talent that gets impacted, and they end up leaving, whereas the average Joe is more than happy to hang around. This is not a way to create a high-performing team. Don't run your department like the Royal Family where everyone's fate has been predetermined and sealed, and people are just waiting for the person in front of them to die or leave. Be deliberate about making changes and moving people around. Create opportunities. I'm not saying this is easy, or that you need to shuffle people all at once, but think about ways you can introduce change to give people opportunities so they can succeed.

☀

Develop effective rituals.

All of us have rituals that obviously affect us directly, like brushing our teeth in the shower to save time (don't judge). But there are others we don't realize provide balance to people outside ourselves and become part of *their* rituals. In short, think twice before you change them.

I remember once canceling a staff meeting because I didn't have much to share. Since I'd already met with my team quite a bit that week, I thought we could forgo the meeting and they could use the time otherwise. Well, when I did that a number of things became clear to me:

* I disrupted the entire team because the staff meeting for many of them was the only meeting they attended based upon their level.

* Because the meeting was a place for my team to share and ask questions as well as get clarification on various projects we were working on or company news, I killed that opportunity.

* The staff meeting was the one place for team members to communicate with each other and voice their views and opinions—not to mention show off what they were working on and what business problems they were solving.

* The meeting was the link for everyone to connect as a team and when I canceled it, it broke their collaboration chain.

The moral of this Davidism is not to cancel routine activities, like staff meetings, if you can help it. They're part of your team's ritual, and they count on them for more reasons than you may know.

Shorts

Assume you could be wrong.

My kids would get a kick out of this one (and so would my husband). It took me a very long time to be comfortable with the notion I could possibly be wrong, and once I reconciled with this far-fetched idea, I truly believe I became a better person, a better listener, and a better manager overall. Ask my team, if you dare.

Enjoy a healthy dose of competition.

When you get promoted or win an award, don't let your guard down. This is not the time to relax. Trust me, there is always someone out there looking to take your lunch. So, never get relaxed if or when you think you have won. That is the time to work even harder.

Be a selfless leader.

As a leader, you should have an "it's not about me" attitude. It's about the people and their hard work. Their dedication got you where you are and will get you where you want to go if you treat them right.

Don't spark up the computer – yet.

Before you sit down at your computer, prioritize and strategize how you are going to spend your day. If you don't, you will spend the day answering emails and chasing down requests from people who need you to help them get *their* work done. At the end of the day, you will likely be exhausted and have nothing to show for it.

Stay in bed.

As I said before, when you can boast that you can do your job with your eyes closed, keep them closed and stay in bed because it's time to look for another job. When you reach this stage, you are definitely no longer using your brain.

Save your pride.

Never be proud of the fact that you are the only one who knows how to do something. This strategy will hold you back from opportunities that may come your way, and it will keep others from learning.

Provide opportunities.

Adding value should be something you do every day —as a manager, it's your duty to provide opportunities for your team to add their value.

Make every task worth doing.

Don't be that person who asks for something and the next thing you know, the entire department drops everything because you had a whim of a request. Be sensitive to the fact that they are working hard and don't need a barrage of interruptions.

Make genuine time for people.

This really goes without saying, but I'll say it anyway. Make genuine time to listen with eye contact and empathy when your employees are speaking to you. Don't be restless and glancing at the clock. And try not to book a meeting with an employee up against another important meeting. Instead, give yourself some space to digest the conversation and to not rush the person in your presence.

☼

Be fair but stern.

A person named Marvin once worked for me and made me a sign that said "Fair but Stern." What he meant by that was I treated everyone the same. For example, if two employees came in separately to ask for the same thing, I would give the same response. I would also put my team before myself, which my team not only expected, but respected me for.

☼

Don't run a democracy.

This might sound like I don't support weighing everyone's voice fairly, but there comes a point where as a leader, it's your responsibility to be decisive and make a decision already. Yes, it's great to let people give their ideas and discuss their recommendations and such, but remember: every decision has to be made, but not every decision has to be voted on.

☼
Offer unsolicited feedback.

At the end of the year, seek out a manager to give them feedback about one of their employees. Don't wait to be asked, and if you are asked to do so by someone, think of it as a privilege.

☼
Embrace managerial courage.

A manager (thank you, Jack!) I worked for early in my career wrote on my performance assessment that I had "managerial courage." When I asked him what he meant by that, he said, "You're not fearful of making a point, you're courageous enough to disagree with me and others, and you're not scared to act." I urge you to embrace the same qualities.

☼
Be relentless about following up.

This one's a no-brainer but merits mentioning: Always return a phone call (except to telemarketers). I am still shocked when I call or email someone back and they are surprised I did. It's called respect.

☀
Fail fast.

In relation to driving your career forward, "fail fast" means that after you've tried the same method of getting a promotion and some time has passed, stop repeating it; instead, try another way and stop spending an enormous amount of time on something that isn't working.

☀
Don't be selfish.

If there's not a path for you, make one so that the person behind you has one to take. Don't be that person who says, "Well, no one helped me." That's just dumb.

☀
If something smells, it stinks.

You've most certainly been in a situation where you knew something was fishy and you brushed it off. Well, I'm here to tell you to go with your gut. Your gut is always right.

The Best Advice I Never Got That I Want You to Have—and Give Away

While I am immensely thankful for the guidance and advice from numerous people throughout my career, I really wish someone had given me the tips that follow before I entered the corporate world. My hope is that you can apply some of these tips to your own career, but even more importantly, I hope you can share them with someone who's behind you on the lifeline.

Popcorn Round (with butter and salt, of course)

*   Your bar should always be higher than your boss's. This will allow you to perform higher than he/she expects.

*   Play checkers with your career—find someone who knows the person you want to meet and have a three-way (easy folks, keep this G-rated!).

* My dad always said, "Where there's a will, there's a relative." But in business, where there's a will, there really is a way.

* Think of everything you do as a business proposition and focus, focus, focus on the problem. What I mean by this is to have a business mindset when you are solving a problem—it helps get rid of the clutter or noise and also take any emotion out of the situation.

* You should never be the only winner in a negotiation, especially if you're negotiating something you want (a raise, training, flexibility, etc.). This means you should never make your request solely about you. The firm, your manager, or your team should be the shared beneficiary of whatever you are asking for.

* You have two ears and one mouth, which means it's important to listen, not necessarily to respond. This is particularly true when your coaches are giving you advice and feedback, or during a performance evaluation or discussion when your boss gives you feedback you don't necessarily agree with, or worse, you vehemently *disagree* with. Take it all in but don't let your mouth take over. Your response should always wait

another day, after you process what is said and have calmed down.

* One-click solutions are best, which is another way of saying, keep things simple. Refrain from developing big, complicated solutions to something, and instead think of easy-to-execute, practical ways to solve a problem.

* Think apple (the fruit, not the company). When you think of an apple, picture a core to remind yourself what the core function of your role is. Then, make sure every decision you make, especially the difficult ones, are grounded in whatever the core functions or tenets of your role are.

* Get behind the strategy of your line of business. Make it your mission to address an aspect of it every single day. Put it on your calendar, and make sure the meetings you hold, the conferences you attend, and the work you distribute to your team all supports the strategy.

* Know when to go. When it's time to move on, get out of the way and free up your space for someone else.

* Never go through an entire PowerPoint presentation in the room. It's better to send

the deck ahead as a pre-read, then focus your time on any specific questions people have or agreements you want to get from the meeting. (Too bad I didn't know this sooner. I spent oodles of time early in my career being a master PowerPoint slide creator, with all the bells and whistles—charts, transitions, sound, timing, and even the right colors and font size so that a person in the back of the room could see the words. It was a thing of beauty, but ultimately, not the best use of my time.)

* Delegate, delegate, delegate.

* Speak with authority and project in staff meetings to make sure you are heard.

* Vet issues with key stakeholders before a big meeting. This way you have friendlies, or a mole, in the room.

* Be decisive. According to Yogi Berra, "If there's a fork in the road, take it." Get it? Most people don't hesitate when decisions are easy, but when the choices are difficult— between two great candidates or two great ideas, for example—people often procrastinate. It's as if waiting long enough will present another variable and make it easier to choose. Many times, however, the

variables won't change, and waiting longer is simply not a good strategy.

* If you don't like what you see, change where you are standing.

* Do a few things really well instead of a lot of things mediocre (this is also helpful in the kitchen!).

* Don't walk. Run and take someone with you.

* Remember you can't get to second unless you get to first. Yes, sometimes it's okay to play small ball and take it slow. (That was not meant to sound like advice to a couple on prom night!) Being on a team, have an attitude of "us" not "me." At times you may be on the bench or not play at all, but your team still needs your support. Depending on what's going on, someone may be stronger in an area than you are and therefore needs to be in a stronger position for the team to win. You need to be okay with that. If you're not, I recommend you get off the team and go play an individual sport.

* Remember the two P's: patience and perseverance. Never give up. Never!

Final Thoughts

I would be lying if I said writing this book was a fun, life-changing experience. In truth, while I was creating it, I found myself coming up with more and more Davidisms that never seemed to end! Whether that means a Part II is on the horizon or not, I hope this book helped you in some way to find *your* way. Every decision you make has an impact on your future, and I sincerely hope reading this book had a positive one. That was certainly my intention. The possibilities for what you can achieve are endless, so don't let anyone make you feel otherwise. As you go through life, have conviction in and for yourself—and whatever you do, don't call 1-800-PAT-DAVID.

Yes, that was meant to be funny, but here's the true story on that.

At the end of a mentoring session or after making a speech, I would often say, "If you ever need to reach me, just call 1-800-PAT-DAVID." It sounded memorable and was kind of a cool way to end a conversation, but I had never actually dialed the number. As I was writing this book, though, I thought, *What the heck, let me dial it and see where it leads.* (Yes, it has one extra number, but it works anyway). Here's what happened:

> **Operator voice:** If you are over 50, please press 1 (so I did).

> **A nice person replied:** Thank you for calling the medical alert center . . .

> At that point I hung up.

> On another occasion I dialed and got:

> This is America's hottest chat line. Press 1 for ladies and 2 for men. Yikes!

So please, I repeat, *please* DO NOT CALL 1-800-PAT-DAVID.

Acknowledgments

Throughout my illustrious career (someone used this to describe me and I liked the way it sounded), there have been many people who have made me *me*—family, friends, co-workers, bosses, passersby, too many to name. If you read this book, you know who you are. Thank You.

My parents were hugely influential in putting into my head that I could do and be anything. For years, as I became successful, I remembered the sacrifice they made to provide the best life and future for their kids. I also cherished their particular brands of wisdom. My dad was fond of saying:

"Don't overstay your welcome or you won't be welcome to overstay again."

"Where there's a will, there's a relative."

"One man's meat is another man's poison."

"The early bird catches the worm. The early worm gets eaten."

"Everything is good in moderation."

"The fruit doesn't fall from the tree—except if the tree is on a hill."

"Make sure the food is hot."

"If I hear all that noise in the kitchen, I'm expecting the food to taste great."

"Hit me!" (referring to pouring more wine into his glass)

And my mom, who was always my mentor and advocate, had one she said so often, we kids joked we'd put it on her headstone:

"Did you eat?"

Who Is Pat David?

PATRICIA DAVID was born in Birmingham, England, after her parents migrated there from the Commonwealth of Dominica. She came to the US in a breadbasket (which is probably why she likes bread—she's grateful she didn't travel in a laundry basket!) and became a naturalized citizen at the age of seven. As a child, she looked like Buckwheat from *The Little Rascals*. If she writes another book, she's already got the title: *From Buckwheat to Wall Street*. Kind of catchy if you ask her.

After growing up in the South Bronx and graduating from Cardinal Spellman High School, where she was the first black captain of the twirling team, she attended Fordham University's Gabelli School of Business, earning a BS in finance and economics, with a minor in accounting, in 1981. She was honored with the installation of the Patricia David Trailblazer Award in 2015 (she says there is nothing cooler than having an award named after you) and later, in 2016, received an honorary Doctorate of Humane Letters.

Pat has held corporate positions with Philip Morris, Merrill Lynch, Salomon Brothers, Citigroup, and JPMorgan Chase, from which she retired as head of diversity in 2018. In 2020 she joined the board of Guiding Eyes for the Blind —an organization that provides guide dogs to people with vision loss.

In her retirement, Pat keeps busy as a professional coach and diversity consultant. She has also learned how to sew (personalized slippers and reversible tote bags for family and friends are her specialty), continues to improve on her West Indian cooking, and spends as much time with her husband, a former Marine, and two grown children as they allow.

Pat currently lives in New Jersey. She is a lifelong fan of the New York Yankees, loves any movie with Denzel Washington, and enjoys *Jeopardy*, crossword puzzles, helping people, and talking—lots of talking.

Awards and Recognition

YWCA – Black Achievers in Industry, March 2002.

YWCA Women Achievers, November 2005. (Privately, it always bothered her that she was awarded Black Achiever before she was awarded Women Achiever. She knows for a fact that when she was born, the doctor did not say, "Congratulations, Mr. and Mrs. LeBlanc, it's black." Her mother actually gave birth to her at home, and she's pretty sure she said, "It's a girl!")

The GlassHammer – Spotlight on People, October 2007.

Induction into the Spellman College Academy of Game Changers, 2012.

Honoree of *The Network Journal* as one of 25 Influential Black Women in Business, 2012.

One of the Top 100 Most Influential Blacks in Corporate America by *Savoy Magazine*.

Black Enterprise – Top Diversity Executive, May 2014.

(One day, she hopes to add a Wife or Mother of the Year Award to this list.)

Pat's Lifelong Motto

If you don't want something done, whatever you do, DON'T GIVE IT TO ME.

Work with Pat

If you could use Pat's services as a great listener to help you move your career along, visit her website to explore the services she offers:

www.patricia-david.com

Connect with Pat

patriciadavidconsulting@gmail.com
LinkedIn: linkedin.com/in/patricia-david-a3660347
Instagram: @patdavid_herstory

Reviews carry a lot of weight for authors.
If you enjoyed *The 'Her'story of Davidisms*, it would mean a lot
if you would leave a favorable review for the book on
Amazon, Barnes & Noble, and/or Goodreads.

If you're able to take the time to review the book—or to buy a
copy for someone you know who could benefit from it—it
would make me very happy!

Many thanks,

Pat